The Making of

The Sound of Music

The Making of
The Sound of Music

MAX WILK

Routledge
Taylor & Francis Group
New York   London

Routledge
Taylor & Francis Group
270 Madison Avenue
New York, NY 10016

Routledge
Taylor & Francis Group
2 Park Square
Milton Park, Abingdon
Oxon OX14 4RN

Printed in the United States of America on acid-free paper
10 9 8 7 6 5 4 3 2 1

International Standard Book Number-10: 0-415-97935-8 (Softcover) 0-415-97934-X (Hardcover)
International Standard Book Number-13: 978-0-415-97935-1 (Softcover) 978-0-415-97934-4 (Hardcover)

Visit the Taylor & Francis Web site at
http://www.taylorandfrancis.com

and the Routledge Web site at
http://www.routledge.com

Contents

Introduction
The Sound of Music

Or, Never Argue with a Hit, no matter how much you hate the show. Remember, if it sells out, the audience is never wrong!

These are the major theatrical lessons that I learned many years back, in those days when I was gainfully employed in the office of Leland Hayward, the brilliant theatrical producer who joined with Mary Martin and her husband, Richard Halliday, in the production of *The Sound of Music*.

Hayward had originally been one of the brightest and most successful talent agents in Hollywood. His list of clients consisted of such major stars as Katharine Hepburn, Henry Fonda, Fred Astaire, Jimmy Stewart, and practically anyone you wish to remember when you turn on Turner Classic Movies tonight.

When Hayward decided to come east from Hollywood and to become a theatrical producer, it was because after all those years in Hollywood he had become convinced of one fact. " I cannot possibly make as many mistakes as all those guys who call themselves producers, can I?" he demanded.

So after opening an office in Manhattan, the new producer quickly succeeded in proving his point ... over and over again. He revealed that talent and class were his passions, and over the years his ever-growing list of successful plays would include *A Bell For Adano, Mr. Roberts*, and many other hits. Musicals? Irving Berlin's *Call Me Madam*, with Ethel Merman. Then he rapidly moved into the new world of live television. He brought to home audiences one of the very first TV spectacles, "The Ford 50th Anniversary," in which Merman and Mary Martin provided their audience a superb performance of a brilliant duet. If you can find it on DVD today, treat yourself to a marvelous performance by those two great singers enjoying themselves for you and the audience. It is unforgettable, and an example of true Hayward showmanship.

Such a successful producer as he'd become meant that his phone never stopped ringing, and all the New York agents would submit their latest plays directly to Leland, ahead of anyone else. So when you walked into his Madison Avenue office, you would always find stacks of new scripts piled high on his desk, waiting patiently to be read. Some fortunate scripts might actually reach the point where Leland read them himself. But most he would parcel out to others in his office, to be read by either his general manager, or an assistant, or whoever else happened to be employed by Hayward on some current project.

I was one of those. I had been added to Hayward's payroll a year or so before, to participate in the preparation of a two-hour TV special that CBS would be presenting in the fall of 1960. "The Fabulous Fifties," as Hayward's productions always were, was a massive project that would please its audiences with an all-star cast — Jackie Gleason, Rex Harrison, Julie Andrews, Henry Fonda, and dozens more. The program was designed to document for the audience everything that had taken place in our land in the past decade. A huge undertaking indeed!

As one of the writers of this two-hour show, I spent many months in the Hayward office, getting the show ready for its debut. That's when I also become one of Leland's sounding boards.

"Kid," he said, one day, "you have a very sharp story mind. You obviously inherited it from your old man. He was a guy with one of the best story minds I ever ran into."

Such a compliment from a shrewd mind such as his was worth cherishing. He knew that my father, Jake Wilk, had been the Warner Brothers story editor for more than three decades. They had done a good deal of business together. Hayward had sold him Edna Ferber's *Saratoga Trunk*, and my father's acumen had brought Warner such classics as *The Maltese Falcon* and *Casablanca*, *I Am a Fugitive from a Chain Gang*, *Now Voyager*, *Yankee Doodle Dandy*, and dozens of other hits.

Leland's compliment would also mean that every so often he would toss a script from one of the desk piles onto my desk, and then suggest I take it home to read it … and return the following day with an opinion on the work.

He would listen to my opinion and nod his head when I gave him my brief rundown of whatever play he'd assigned to me. His questions about the script were always sharp and to the point. During that time, he was not only supervising that massive television project, but he was also engaged in producing a new musical destined for Broadway. It would be based on the life story of Gypsy Rose Lee, her sister June, and their mother, Mrs.

Hovick. It would be directed by the choreographer Jerry Robbins, and it would be set to the music and lyrics of Jule Styne and Steven Sondheim. It was designed to be a starring vehicle for Ethel Merman.

Not a bad layout, indeed.

Then came one memorable afternoon when, after all those months of preparation, arguments, discussions and the inevitable back-and-forth fights that go into the preparation of a Broadway musical, there would be the first Sunday afternoon run-through of *Gypsy* at the Winter Garden Theatre. Here an excited audience of theatrical people on their days off would be treated to the first bare-stage performance of this incredible undertaking.

"You better be there," Leland instructed, and added, "Bring your wife along, I want to know how she likes it too. Just remember, the show may need work, but it's going to get it, trust me. But it's so much damn work," he sighed. "There are times when I'd like just to quit the whole damn thing and forget about it. But I can't," he continued, "it's got so much stuff going for it. Who knows? We just might have ourselves a hit."

That Sunday afternoon the Winter Garden was packed.

The lights came up on the bare stage. There we saw a group of kids being auditioned for an amateur kiddy show. One of those kids was Louise, one of the two Hovick sisters. As she came out on the bare stage to begin her audition, singing "Let Me Entertain You," there came from the back of the theatre a stentorian, unmistakable voice. "Sing out, Louise!" she cried, as down the aisle came Ethel Merman, clutching a small dog in her arms. And the entire Winter Garden audience rose to give a roar of welcome to their star!

Who could forget such an afternoon?

The following morning Leland called me into his office. Okay, how had I liked the run-through? What did my wife and I think about *Gypsy*?

How could I explain to him that Barbara and I had gone home so high with excitement that we both agreed we'd probably never forget the matinee? Nor have we.

"Probably one of the best musicals we've ever seen," I assured him.

"Oh boy, do I hope you're both right, " sighed Leland. And suddenly so did I, because I knew, such is the capriciousness of show business, we might end up being wrong.

When *Gypsy* opened, thankfully, the critics would agree with our enthusiasm. And when "The Fabulous Fifties" aired on CBS, the response was remarkably affirmative. So things were going just fine in the Hayward office — that is, until *The Sound of Music* went into production.

It had been Mary Martin's decision to bring Leland in as the show's producer, and Leland agreed enthusiastically. Had he not been fortunate with

Ethel Merman in *Gypsy*? Certainly, with this musical saga of the Trapp family, Mary Martin would do as well.

Leland began to spend many hours in meetings with that marvelous team of veteran Broadway playwrights, Howard Lindsay and Russel Crouse, who had already begun to work on the script. Rodgers and Hammerstein were delayed with their work on the musical score, but that did not impede the forward motion of *The Sound of Music*. Meanwhile, Leland continued getting the script ready. Since the Lindsay and Crouse team were doing such a good job, he exuded optimism with each passing meeting. And when Rodgers and Hammerstein finally became free to work on the music and lyrics, how could such a project not be successful?

"It's going to be a smash," he promised. "Mary is perfect for this part. Can't you feel it coming?"

No, actually, I did not.

I couldn't explain why, but for some reason — as much as I had enjoyed Mary Martin over all those years since she first knocked the audience in the New Haven Shubert for a loop when she did a duet with Gene Kelly, "My Heart Belongs To Daddy," or later, "That's Him" as an adoring lover in *One Touch of Venus* — the truth was, I somehow couldn't envision her as Maria, the religious lady who comes from the nunnery to work in the Trapp family home, and who eventually joins the Trapps in their journey to safety.

But whenever Leland would enthusiastically bring up some new scene or quote the lyrical ideas that were beginning to emerge from Oscar Hammerstein's fertile mind, I knew enough to keep quiet. For some reason, Leland was too smart not to sense that I didn't care for his newest project. Why was I so reluctant to discuss it?

I had to tell the truth. It simply did not feel like my dish of tea.

"Okay," he said. "But that doesn't mean you're not coming to the first run-through. I need your ideas."

When that event was scheduled, it would be in a small theater — now gone — on 43rd Street, on a warm August afternoon. Once again Barbara joined me, and we proceeded up to the mezzanine. We sat with an audience anxious and excited to see this new Rodgers and Hammerstein venture. Why not? Were they not the greatest team of songwriters of our time? So on it came, again on a bare stage.

When it was all over, and we'd heard their new score and digested the Lindsay and Crouse book, it all seemed serviceable. Mary Martin and Theo Bikel, her leading man, seemed well suited for their parts. But somehow we were not excited. Was it perhaps the music and lyrics? "My Favorite Things," "The Sound of Music," "Do Re Mi," "Sixteen, Going on Seventeen," et al., were truly professional. And the Trapp family's departure from Europe to safety? And the love story between Trapp and Maria? Of course, it was the necessary happy ending.

So why hadn't we enjoyed it?

It's hard to recall the exact reason why we both made our way through the crowded Henry Miller Theatre lobby with no elation whatsoever.

And then came the moment when Leland followed us out into 43rd Street to insist on our reactions.

I had to lie. I needed time to digest what I had seen and heard, and so, I insisted, did Barbara.

Leland shook his head. "You're both ducking me," he said finally. He hadn't spent all those years in and out of Hollywood previews not to recognize the truth of our reactions. But he wasn't buying it. Not from either of us.

"I think it would be a good idea if you both came up to New Haven to the opening at the Shubert," he said firmly. "You'll both get a better idea of what this show can be, okay? So plan it for that night, understood?" And he departed to find some other lobby guest whose brain could be picked.

"Must we sit through it *again*?" asked Barbara.

"Yes, I think so," I told her. "After all, I am working for the man, aren't I? And we can get from Ridgefield to the Shubert in forty minutes." Remember, that was half a century ago — B.T. (Before Traffic).

The opening night in New Haven was October 3, 1959.

The theatre had been sold out days before. One announcement of Mary Martin's newest show, with its score by Rodgers and Hammerstein, had cleaned out the box office completely. Barbara and I had long since hired our babysitter so that we were free to leave Ridgefield in time to make the opening night curtain.

We should have been excited. The theatre was packed with all sorts of show business luminaries. Press people and Hollywood names filled the rows of seats behind and around us. As we filed in, we encountered Leland in the lobby. "Just remember," he warned me, "when it's all over, you and I need to talk. Understood?"

I nodded. We went to our seats. "What are you going to tell him?" murmured my wife. I really didn't know. I crossed my fingers. Perhaps these theatrical wizards had tuned up their show into something wonderful? Why not?

The orchestra struck up the overture, and then we were off on Maria Trapp's journey.

On and on came the songs: "Climb Ev'ry Mountain," "Edelweiss," "How Can Our Love Survive." It was mostly the same score as the one we'd heard that afternoon weeks back. Oh yes, now there were scenery and costumes, and Mary Martin was, as usual, enchanting, and Theo Bikel was her fine leading man.

But one of my California producer friends, seated in the row ahead of us, turned around at one point, shook his head, and rolled his eyes. And I knew just what that meant. He was hating it too!

"Climb Every Mountain" soared out ... and finally, it was over.

Waves of applause rose from the New Haven audience, while Barbara and I moved swiftly up the aisle. The cast was still taking bows onstage. It was a trick I'd learned from my father — to get out before the mob left and avoid any discussion. Tonight I was practicing his rule to avoid Leland, who'd insist on picking my brain.

We struggled out through the Shubert lobby, then out to the New Haven street ahead of the crowd. But as we were on our way to the parking garage to pick up our car and make a getaway, I heard Leland calling me. Damn! I thought I'd made it, but I hadn't. He caught up with us.

"Okay," he insisted, pinning me against the outside wall. "What's the verdict?"

"We have got go home and relieve a babysitter!" I pleaded.

"Don't try ducking out," he said. "I brought you both up here so you could tell me what you think of this show!"

I had to tell him the truth. I took a deep breath. "It's just not my kind of show," I insisted.

"Then be specific!" he demanded. "What the hell don't you like?"

How could I confess that I had spent most of the evening writhing through those waves of treacle that had poured across the Shubert footlights? Obviously, I'd have to find something specific to hate! Leland would accept nothing less.

"Those two songs the couple does in the second act?" I suggested desperately. "They don't seem to belong in this show at all. Especially that one they do, 'How Can our Love Survive.'"

"And what else?" Leland persisted.

"I don't really know anything else," I lied.

"But you hate it, right? And how about you, Barbara?" Leland asked. "You agree with him."

"Absolutely," said my wife.

"Okay," said Leland. "That does it. Thanks for coming." And he disappeared into the crowd.

"Whew!" said my wife as we drove back to Ridgefield. "Glad that's over."

"No it isn't. Not yet," I said grimly. "I have to go into the office tomorrow, remember?"

The next morning Leland did not show up, which meant that his third degree would be postponed. When he finally appeared, he called me in and closed the door. "I've been thinking about what you both said last night," he said. "You both have a right to hate the show, even if you can't tell me specifically why. But I have one thing it would help you to learn right now. Whether you or your wife, or even the New York critics, hate this show, I got the feeling that the audience last night loved it. And when that happens, Max, don't ever argue with the audience. Go get this motto written on a plaque and hang it on your wall in big type. It's the only truth that matters about a show, believe me." He handed me a piece of paper on which I read: "NOBODY LIKES IT BUT THE PEOPLE." Leland waved a finger at me. "Trust me. That is absolutely all that counts."

All these years later, after dozens of other opening nights and tryouts and run-throughs and reruns, I've seen how Leland's motto is the only truth you can trust in this peculiar world we persist in calling "show business."

The Sound of Music later began its triumphal run in Manhattan and then ran many years on tour. There's no need to go through a litany of the mediocre reviews it received over those years.

We never seemed able to avoid it. When we moved our family to London during the 1960s, there it was. It had opened at the huge Palace Theatre in 1961, and it would play there until January 1967, for a total of 2,385 performances. When the film version made by Twentieth Century Fox opened in 1965 at a theatre a few blocks away from the Palace, one would have assumed that the film version would eventually close down the Palace production.

No such thing! British audiences flocked to both venues quite regularly. It did not matter a bit that they had already enjoyed the live production. They wanted to enjoy it again, and week after week all through the sixties, there were those two venues, running in downtown London. As if to taunt us, perhaps?

It did not seem to matter that Harold Hobson of the prestigious *Sunday Times* had originally written, "It is a mistake to treat the von Trapps as heroes. ... This falsity of feeling undermines the whole entertainment. ... Far and away the best thing in the evening is Rodgers' music. ... It is like Moody and Sanky soused in sugar." But he added somewhat ruefully, "*The Sound of Music* is going to be one of the biggest successes of all time."

On and on ran the show, after 2,385 performances the longest-running American musical ever to play in London, while week after week, loyal fans kept cheerfully buying tickets to the Fox film version.

Some years after *The Sound of Music* had begun its triumphal run, we were back in America, and it was obvious that the Fox film version would continue to run and run to please the audiences, even after all these years.

I dropped into Leland's office a few years after the original production had opened. He had kept himself busy producing various plays, one of them *The Trial of the Catonsville Nine*, a drama, not a musical, quite the opposite of the saga of the Trapp family.

That day Leland's desk was, as usual, covered with all sorts of paper, but with one very visible difference. These were not the usual piles of play-scripts, waiting for him or one of his assistants to read. No, these were white bank checks — quite a lot of them spread out all over Leland's desk. At a cursory glance, they might add up to seventy or eighty.

As usual, the Hayward phone kept ringing, and Miss Malley, his faithful secretary, kept announcing various important phone calls, which seemed to interrupt what Leland was busily doing — finishing signing these assembled checks made out to various names.

"Do you know who's getting all these checks?" he asked me, grinning.

No, I had to confess I did not.

"Well," said Leland, "these are payments to all of those backers who invested in a show you may remember from some years back, when it opened up at the Shubert in New Haven. Do you recall that night? You and your wife were there."

"*The Sound of Music*," I said.

"Exactly," said Leland. "And since we have just received this new payment of one million dollars and change for the backers from a settlement, I seem to be in charge of distributing, as I have for the past ten years, and sending them all their share of this money."

I had thought if I left London and returned to the States we would finally get away from *The Sound of Music*. But obviously we hadn't!

"How very nice for you and those faithful backers," I managed to say.

Leland grinned cheerfully, resembling nothing more than a middle-aged Cheshire cat.

"Not bad," he shrugged, "considering that it is a show which has never gotten a decent review, eh?"

He was absolutely right.

And that is why I have never forgotten the rule he taught me, which I now again pass on to you: *NEVER ARGUE WITH A HIT.*

Max Wilk

November 29, 2005

CHAPTER 1

Scene Changes

Sixteen years had passed.

Sixteen theatre seasons since that memorable *Away We Go!* opening night, since the curtain of New Haven's Shubert Theatre had risen and the lights had revealed a bright, sun-drenched Oklahoma landscape where Aunt Eller sat silently churning her butter.

Not a sound. And then the bemused Shubert audience had heard, offstage, the sound of Alfred Drake's voice singing "Oh, What a Beautiful Mornin'."

Who had known that it was not only a theatrical opening that night, but the premiere of a revolutionary era? That from then on, in the American musical theatre, the scene would keep changing?

Gone, mostly, were those comedian-driven roughhouse musicals of the late 1920s and 1930s. Vanished were the opulent, slightly risqué *Scandals* and *Vanities,* and *Follies,* and other such displays, revues with their parades of beautiful half-dressed damsels, designed to please the tired businessman seated on the aisle down front. Such shows had been replaced by satire, by characterizations, set to clever lyrics-cum-melody that impelled empathetic laughter at man's foibles. Comedy was growing up, accompanied by songs that had not been dropped into a show by haphazard interpolation but that needed to be up there for a reason, usually to serve the plot.

Operettas? Those were on the shelf, or stored away in the Shubert warehouse. Perhaps you could still enjoy a Romberg or a Friml revival out at the St. Louis Municipal Opera, or encounter it on tour in the hinterlands, but as far as New York was concerned, after *Oklahoma!* innovation was the order of the day.

Where once the 45th and 46th Street musical stages had echoed to the sound of tap dancing, now choreography reigned. (Leave it to Irving Berlin to spoof the new trend with his sardonic "Choreography," in 1954.) With Agnes de Mille leading the way, choreographers of the skill and talent of Jerome Robbins, Gower Champion, Michael Kidd, and Danny Daniels followed. And later, Bob Fosse, Ron Field, and Michael Bennett would become primary forces in creating musicals.

So strong was de Mille's influence that there is a satiric barb, a truly inside joke, in the book of the 1958 musical, *Say, Darling,* when a Harold Prince-type producer is auditioning dancers for a new musical production. One hapless dancer arrives for his audition and launches into a rapid-fire tap dance. He's promptly interrupted by the stage manager, calling "*Thank you—next!*" And the poor frustrated hoofer comes down front, to yell out at us "Damn it, doesn't *anybody* want tap dancing?"

Subtext: Damn you, Agnes!

Truth in character, strong plot line, and that second-act ballet were the order of the day. But musical tickets were still sold by stars. So there would still be shows that harkened back to the formulaic days when Ed Wynn ("The Perfect Fool"), Al Jolson, Eddie Cantor ("Banjo Eyes"), or Marilyn Miller ("Sunny") would bring out the Standing Room Only sign.

For the producers, there were, fortunately, a few holdover stars from the 1930s and 1940s who could still carry a musical and keep the box-office telephones ringing: Ethel Merman, out there "in one" — spotlighted in front of the traveler curtain — belting out a solo crafted to order for her by Cole Porter. Or she would make the Imperial Theatre's rafters echo (unamplified, thank you) with the amazing score provided by her reliable friend, Irving Berlin. His *Annie Get Your Gun* was proof positive of her ability to carry a two-hour show and to keep the customers coming back for more — just as, a few seasons later, she would knock audiences for a loop as Rose, in *Gypsy.*

Were there still funny men? Yes, a few. Raffish, "wowoweeweewoh!" guys, such as Phil Silvers, who, equipped with a great second banana, the inexhaustible Joey Faye, could romp through such an old-fashioned exhibit as *High Button Shoes,* delivering belly laughs interwoven with the Jule Styne–Sammy Cahn score, and its vaudeville-style soft-shoe dance numbers. (Even that show's choreographer, Jerome Robbins, would modify his inevitable second-act ballet so that it would be pure low comedy based on Mack Sennett's classic slapstick bathing-beauties-by-the-sea two-reelers.) And we still had Bert Lahr, a remarkably gifted clown, who could keep his audiences happy by growling, roaring, gargling, and double-taking throughout such smorgasbords of shtick as *Two on the Aisle* or *Foxy.* Sooner or later, when such vehicles disappeared, Lahr would switch to drama. (When he and another gifted clown, Tom Ewell, ended up in Samuel Beckett's *Waiting for Godot* sans music and lyrics, they may not have known precisely what Beckett's script *meant,* but no one who saw them could deny they knew how to *play* it.)

There were, blessedly, a few new talents around, such as the wonderful Nancy Walker, who brought with her echoes of the knockabout vaudeville era. (Her father had been a trouper before she'd arrived on the scene.) And for the remarkable Judy Holliday Broadway could still find vehicles; she starred in *Bells Are Ringing,* and who is to say how much further she might have traveled, had she not departed so soon from our musical stage?

Yes, echoes of the old-fashioned musical could still be encountered in the shows that leaned heavily toward comedy, as did *Pajama Game,* and *Damn Yankees,* done by the master, George Abbott. But as the seasons passed, even Mr. Abbott found it harder and harder to bring forth musical hits. With all those tried and true show-stopping elements fading away, experimentation become the order of the day ... or of the closing night. Dozens of productions would fall by the wayside as hapless librettists and their songwriting teams labored at being smart, or clever, or satiric.

Every so often a new talent would emerge, such as Frank Loesser, who'd been working out in Hollywood. He brashly insisted he was capable of emulating Porter and Berlin by providing both music and lyrics. And starting with his sparkling *Where's Charley?* Loesser proved he could knock them out of the ballpark for the next two decades. But for every Loesser who emerged in those confused times, the Broadway arena was strewn with the corpses of failed musicals. We weren't waiting for Godot; we were waiting for Lerner and Loewe, and until they arrived there were all sorts of high-cost attempts that began life as innovations, closed, and can only be remembered in the bins of record shops that specialize in rare LPs.

Where was the American musical headed?

Or was it headed anywhere at all? If heretofore successful practitioners such as Mr. Abbott and others of his generation were frustrated and depressed, bewildered tyros were equally so.

One night in 1951, at a meeting of New Dramatists, the then recently created support group for young playwrights who'd earned their place at the table by having already written and been produced, the two sachems of the day, Mr. Rodgers and Mr. Hammerstein, came to offer their accumulated knowledge and opinions to a room full of intent listeners.

Whatever they had to tell us, it had to be valid. After all, was this not the era of successful Rodgers and Hammerstein musicals? Those Hammerstein librettos, expertly crafted and set to the memorable Rodgers scores? Couldn't we call back those evenings — some perhaps more enchanted than others — of *Carousel* or *Allegro?* Hadn't they provided a lilting score for their movie musical *State Fair*? Their latest show, *The King and I,* with Gertrude Lawrence and Yul Brynner, was a wonderful work. Overall, the Rodgers and Hammerstein partnership ever since *Oklahoma!* had managed to rack up a spectacular batting average.

So successful was the team, in fact, as creators and producers, that a favorite Broadway anecdote of those times dealt with an apocryphal message from the Colonial Theatre, up in Boston, where a billboard had gone up:

Coming! Rodgers and Hammerstein's New Show!

"We grossed twenty-six thousand yesterday," the Colonial manager was supposed to have reported. "But yesterday was Sunday! Your box office wasn't even *open!*" protested the New York reporter. "Yeah, but when the people saw that Rodgers and Hammerstein sign," said the Bostonian, "they pushed open our lobby doors and threw in their checks!"

Hyperbole, perhaps, but based on truth. So strong had been the Rodgers and Hammerstein influence on the American musical since 1943 that the form and structure of all Broadway shows that followed would be compared to their patterns.

During the question-and-answer period which followed that evening at New Dramatists, one of the playwrights, who'd already worked on several musical librettos and was waiting, none too patiently, for a production — any sort of production, in those pre–off-Broadway days — raised his hand: "Mr. Hammerstein," he asked, "nobody can argue, these are bleak days for the musical. Can you foresee any future for those of us who're still trying to work in that field?"

Hammerstein smiled and nodded. "Believe me," he said, "I know exactly how you feel."

And we all knew he had been there, too, in the best of times and the worst of times. There had been all those fallow years he had struggled through before the success of *Oklahoma!*

"The only answer I can give you," said this man who was currently half of the most successful team on Broadway, "is that I firmly believe, right now, as we're talking, somewhere, out there, in a room, there's a guy, maybe two such, working on an idea for a new show. Something exciting, something different, with perhaps a whole new vision of the way a musical can be done. I have to believe this. What he's working on — who knows? Maybe it'll shake us all up and open a whole new way to go."

There was silence as we sat and pondered his prediction of a rosy new future.

"Trust me," Hammerstein promised. "I've been around a long time. It always happens this way."

The room was still silent. His theatrical glass wasn't half empty, it was half full. And who could dare argue with the man who'd already written "A Cock-Eyed Optimist"?

It would take a while for his prediction to come true, but when it did, it proved to be worth waiting for. The work would be called *West Side Story*, a bold, startlingly new vision of Shakespeare's *Romeo and Juliet*, transformed by Arthur Laurents's libretto, set to a vibrant score by Leonard Bernstein, and with lyrics by a brilliant new talent, Stephen Sondheim. Brilliantly directed and choreographed by Jerome Robbins, it had the Broadway musical off and running again, leading us headlong into a bold new era of creativity.

And *West Side Story* (as *Oklahoma!* before it) would do it without a single star name on the marquee. But that was after a lot of time had passed. The Broadway tradition that evening at New Dramatists still was — as it had long been — that of the phenomenal talents who brought in the ticket buyers and kept the shows running. Stars like Mary Martin.

Mary Martin

Indeed, a show business phenomenon had emerged in 1938 on the stage of New Haven's Shubert Theatre (where else?). In the midst of a Cole Porter musical, *Leave It to Me,* there arrived a cheerful young woman attired in a fur parka. Surrounded by chorus boys (one of whom was a young hoofer named Gene Kelly), she launched into one of Porter's cleverest and sauciest set of double-entendre lyrics in the song "My Heart Belongs to Daddy."

By the second chorus, when this lissome actress from Weatherford, Texas, began performing a mock strip-tease with her parka, letting us know it was all in good, not-so-clean fun, the New Haven audience had begun to fall in love with her. When she finished the number, Mary Martin stopped the show — as she would continue to do for many seasons to come. She could sing, she could clown, she could dance. And the audience remained in love with her when she later played a mythical goddess come to life in *One Touch of Venus*. Out in Hollywood, she did a batch of musical films; then she came back to the stage to costar with Noël Coward in *Pacific 1860*.

But her finest hour would come in 1949, when she merged her considerable talents with those of Rodgers and Hammerstein, to play Ensign Nellie Forbush in *South Pacific*, opposite the opera star Ezio Pinza. Those were the evenings — and the matinees — when audiences were enchanted as she showered and shampooed and told us that she was going to wash that man right out of her hair, or did the hilarious cakewalk to "Honey Bun," and finally, promised Pinza that once she had found him, she would never let him go.

Her fans adored her. She could do no wrong.

Especially with that brilliant libretto and score by Rodgers and Hammerstein. *South Pacific* ran in New York for 1,925 performances, and Mary Martin played Nellie for two years. Obviously, Rodgers and Hammerstein would have been delighted to create another such successful musical for her, but it would be eight years before it finally happened. Anyone in the theater knows that lightning rarely strikes twice in the same place, if it strikes at all.

Mary Martin and her husband, Richard Halliday, and Rodgers and Hammerstein went their separate ways, but their tracks remained parallel. Rodgers and Hammerstein were busy over the next few years producing tours of their shows, mounting British productions, and creating new shows: *The King and I, Me and Juliet, Pipe Dream,* an original version of *Cinderella* for television, and *Flower Drum Song.* Their days and nights were occupied.

So were Mary Martin's. She may not have found another *South Pacific* — it would be miraculous to find such an overpowering mixture of showmanship — but she kept busy. She played opposite Charles Boyer in a tissue-thin romantic comedy, *Kind Sir,* by Norman Krasna. Even though the play had a respectable run, it wasn't precisely the sort of show the fans expected. Then such an audience-pleaser happily arrived — a new musical version of Sir James M. Barrie's beloved classic *Peter Pan.*

With her husband as producer and Jerome Robbins as director and choreographer; with a stage full of talented kids and Cyril Ritchard to play the villainous Captain Hook; with a score by Carolyn Leigh and Moose Charlap, plus additional songs by Betty Comden, Adolph Green, and Jule Styne, this revival provided Mary Martin ample opportunity to shine. And when she took off to soar triumphantly across the stage, she wasn't the only one who was flying — her empathetic audiences were flying along with her. They couldn't care less that she was a trifle old to play Peter; they simply knew that they loved her.

As would millions more when she took her performance and re-created it for that fledgling entertainment venue, the twelve-inch television screen. It was Leland Hayward, a shrewd showman and Martin's good friend, who delivered her and *Peter Pan* to NBC as the first in a procession of what he dubbed "spectaculars." *Peter Pan* promptly became a TV classic to be rebroadcast year after year.

Sometimes the best laid plans of producers "gang aft agley," but not as agley as did Mary Martin's next venture. In 1955, someone in the State Department in Washington, D.C., decided it would be a brilliant idea to send a new production of Thornton Wilder's *The Skin of Our Teeth* over to Paris as part of a festival called "A Salute to France." On paper, it all must have sounded marvelous: a cast including Helen Hayes, and the legendary George Abbott returning to the stage as an actor, and, in the role originally created by Tallulah Bankhead, Mary Martin as the outrageous comedienne–maid Sabina. No, it wasn't precisely typecasting, but in the theater such oddball ideas often pan out.

Not this time. *The Skin of Our Teeth* returned from Paris, where it had been less than marvelous, opened in New York, and, after three weeks, closed.

While Martin looked around for another vehicle, one that might involve her good friends Dick and Oscar, she took on the leading role of Annie Oakley in one of their early triumphs as show producers, *Annie Get Your Gun,* first to play it on a national tour, and then in another NBC "spectacular."

And then it happened.

Martin's good friend, director Vincent Donehue, went from staging her production of *Annie Get Your Gun* to working at Paramount, out in Hollywood, where he'd previously been signed to a contract. One day in 1957, he was taken into a projection room where he was shown a German film, *Die Trapp Familie.*

The story of the Baroness Maria von Trapp — who had escaped the Nazi regime with her family, left her native Austria, and come to America, where she and the *kinder* performed as the Trapp Family Singers — the film had been made in Germany a decade before. So successful had it been with German audiences that it had been followed by a sequel, *Die Trapp Familie in Amerika.*

Paramount had secured an option on the rights to these films, and, Donehue was told, someone had the idea to turn the Trapp saga into an American musical. What did he think of the possibility? He thought immediately of one leading lady. Nobody knew better than Donehue how urgently Mary and Dick Halliday had been seeking a starring vehicle. He managed to get the film back east, where he showed it to both of them.

Martin, equally enthusiastic, immediately agreed with Donehue. But how should they proceed? With Paramount owning the option on the story, perhaps they should deal directly with Baroness von Trapp and try to secure the rights to her life story as the basis for a Broadway show.

But the baroness was in New Guinea, involved in missionary work. When she began to receive communications from a group of Americans she'd never heard of, suggesting that her life story might make a musical starring Mary Martin, the baroness ignored them. Who was this Mary Martin? She wished to play her on a theatre stage? *Furicht!*

But when the baroness returned from New Guinea, Halliday was waiting to meet her ship in San Francisco; Martin was playing *Annie Get Your*

Gun in the same city. The baroness would be in the audience that night. Once the curtain had fallen, Halliday brought her backstage to meet the star, and at that point, the saga of *The Sound of Music* began.

Theatrical fantasies always begin with someone's hypothesis — the one we know as *What if?* Most often such fantasies arrive at the end of the runway, where some of them, like Theresa Helburn's folly, take off and fly. But the majority of them, alas, never make it into the air. In this particular *What if?*, the fantasy was not only valid, it would prove to be solid gold.

Mary Martin, to play Maria Reiner, the nun who left her convent to tend to the children of Captain Georg von Trapp, a retired naval officer, and who'd fallen in love with the widower father, and he with her ... and when they'd been married, she'd had more children, creating a large brood of talented young von Trapps ... and when the Nazis had overrun Austria, the parents and the children had left their homeland, escaping to far-off America, where they'd create a new career — she and the children becoming the famous Trapp Family Singers: it was a *What if* that would fly higher than any Austrian Alp.

But not until quite a few legal Alps had been climbed. For starters, Paramount's option on the two Trapp Family films had lapsed; the rights to the story had reverted to the German production company. And nobody could use the baroness's own life story without such rights, because years back, in the original deal she'd agreed to, she'd signed a contract in which she gave over all her rights to her life story, including any and all profit participation, for the magnificent sum of $9,000. So, alas, it would not be up to the baroness whether Mary Martin could re-create her story on a Broadway stage. It would be up to that German film company, which owned all the rights. Negotiations began, and after discussion, the Germans agreed to a deal by which they would sell the rights to Martin and Halliday for $200,000 — far from the original sum paid to the Baroness von Trapp!

Others might have been stopped by such a price, but not Mary Martin and Richard Halliday. When you've found a project you believe is worth doing, and you have the determination to pursue it, then you take a cue from Oscar Hammerstein's words (the ones which were as yet unwritten) — and you climb every mountain.

Even if you don't *have* the $200,000 on hand to pay that German company.

"Dick was a very shrewd businessman," remembered Frank Goodman, who would become the theatrical press agent for the original production of *The Sound of Music*. "He and Mary looked around for capital, and guess how they figured it all out? Mary had a long-term contract with NBC Television. She'd been such a huge hit for them in *Peter Pan*. NBC could run it, year after year, and the kids loved it. In her contract, she also owed them another 'spectacular' each year, at a very good fee. So Dick went over to

Radio City and asked the NBC executives for an advance on Mary's future salary. NBC, of course, wanted to keep their star happy, and they knew Mary would earn back that money for them in the future, so they agreed to lend Mary and Dick the $200,000 so they could use it to finish their deal with the Germans!"

With the NBC funds agreed to, the couple proceeded to close the deal with the German film company for the rights to the two Trapp films, and the rights to the baroness's life story. And even though they were not bound to do so legally, they voluntarily signed over a royalty of three-eighths of one percent to the baroness for the forthcoming show based on her life story. It may not sound like much on a one-week basis, but over the years since 1959, the sum has been impressive.

Then they got in touch with a prospective producer for the project: their tried-and-true friend Leland Hayward.

PARTNERING WITH THE BEST

One of the most successful showmen of his time, Hayward had begun his career in Hollywood as an agent for talent. In the film business, he was legendary as a specialist in class. Eventually he sold his agency to Jules Stein, who founded the movie department at MCA upon it. In times to come, Hayward would regret this sale whenever he entered into a furious negotiation with MCA. "Created my own goddamned monster," he would sigh.

But Hayward had set his sights on moving to New York and producing plays on his own. "I saw all those conceited bastards I dealt with who called themselves producers out there, making so many mistakes," he said later. "I figured I couldn't possibly do any worse than they were doing."

Over the next two decades, Hayward's name went proudly onto the marquees of a long list of Broadway hits, from *Mr. Roberts* to *State of the Union, Wish You Were Here,* and *Call Me Madam.* He'd been partnered with Rodgers and Hammerstein as producers of *South Pacific.* And he had delivered on NBC's *Peter Pan.*

Since nothing succeeds like success, especially in show business where success is so rare, he was Martin and Halliday's first choice.

Hayward looked at the two German films on the von Trapp family and read their biography, too. Did he agree that the part of the baroness was a good one for Mary Martin?

"Absolutely!" he said, cheerfully. "Let's get started!"

The rights deal with the Germans closed, Martin and Halliday were the owners, and Hayward agreed to become their partner. The project began to move forward.

In the beginning, there needed to be a script.

It was agreed that the first choice for the script would be the writing team of Howard Lindsay and Russel Crouse. Hayward had been their agent ever since his Hollywood days, and he'd continued his relationship with them during the creation of Ethel Merman's success *Call Me Madam*. "Leland called," remembered Anna Crouse, Russel's wife. "And he said to Russel and Howard, I have three ideas for you two, and you can have your choice. One is *Gone with the Wind* as a musical, the second is Gypsy Rose Lee's book *Gypsy,* and the third is about the Trapp Family Singers, which Mary has brought me. You decide."

Lindsay and Crouse went into conference.

As a Broadway writer–manager team, two men could not have been more respected and successful. They were two of the wittiest men in the business. Their writing credits went all the way back to the now classic comedy *Life with Father,* in which Lindsay had also starred as the patriarch

Figure 1.1 Producer Leland Hayward. (Courtesy of Photofest)

of the title. When they decided to become producers, they scored with such successes as *Arsenic and Old Lace, The Hasty Heart,* and *Detective Story.*

When Lindsay called Hayward back, he said, "Leland, you'll never get *Gone with the Wind* on a stage — it's not possible, it's too big!"

What about *Gypsy?* "They just didn't feel it was for them," said Mrs. Crouse. "I once had in the office a list of the plays and musicals they'd turned down, and it was quite impressive. Practically every hit you ever knew. But luckily, they told Leland they were very interested in the Mary Martin project."

Hayward promptly arranged for the two writers to read the von Trapp biography, and to see the black-and-white German films. And they began to think about writing the book for the musical.

"Then Leland called," remembered Mrs. Crouse, "and he said, 'You know, I've been thinking about this, and I think the story needs a little *oomph,* and how do you feel about my asking Dick Rodgers and Oscar Hammerstein whether they would write a song or two for this? I mean, we know the von Trapp repertoire is full of German classics, but maybe they ought to do something new, don't you agree?' Well, Russel and Howard said, 'That's great, go ahead and see what they say.' "

"After all," she added, "who wouldn't want Dick and Oscar writing songs for you?"

So Hayward went through the same process with Rodgers and Hammerstein, showing them the book and having the German films run for them.

"Dick called Leland," said Mrs. Crouse, "and he said, 'No way am I competing with Mozart and Brahms and Austrian folksongs — all that stuff they're singing. Oscar and I would like to write the *entire* score.'"

"And why not?" was Hayward's response.

Why not, indeed? Who could turn down Rodgers and Hammerstein?

But there was one proviso. The authors of *South Pacific* would not be available until their current project, *Flower Drum Song,* had been successfully launched — which would be at least a year.

No matter. Martin and Halliday, Hayward, and Lindsay and Crouse would certainly be willing to wait.

CHAPTER **2**

The Libretto

"An audience must go away from your play feeling rewarded ... or purged." That was one of Howard Lindsay's most pragmatic rules for theatrical success.

And certainly no libretto would prove his thesis more reliably than the one he and Russel Crouse had begun to work on during that winter of 1958–59.

For what Lindsay and Crouse accomplished in *The Sound of Music* was the creation of a truly heartwarming story, one that has charmed audiences ever since. No matter that they took certain liberties with the von Trapp saga. Who cares that, in the show, when the von Trapps make their final departure from Salzburg to escape the Nazis and climb the Alps to Switzerland, the geography is askew? Facts don't make a successful show, but rewarding the audience does. The youngsters who sit home today rapt by the videotape of *The Sound of Music* in its film version, or their *fort-confrères* in orchestra seats at Broadway's Martin Beck Theatre in its 1998 revival, or the performers in some little theatre company presenting the show this very night somewhere, all share in the same experience: complete empathy with Maria and her Captain, and those loving von Trapp kids.

Small wonder that time has proven *The Sound of Music* and *Oklahoma!* to be Rodgers and Hammerstein's two most successful musical works.

Ah, but let us pause here just a moment, and consider the anomaly of these two diametrically different Rodgers and Hammerstein musicals! One is grounded on the sunlit American prairie and populated with cowboys and farmers settling the brand-new state of Oklahoma — a thrilling piece that, in its primary execution, broke from most of the formulas of the Broadway of its time.

The other, *The Sound of Music,* is grounded in the Austrian Alps. Well, it's hard to believe that the show that would prove to be, alas, Rodgers and Hammerstein's final collaboration could come from the same creative pair. For *The Sound of Music* is very much in the old vein of operetta — the very source of the formulas that *Oklahoma!* had broken away from. The noble story of a brave heroine, a nun, who falls in love with the middle-aged father of a family and renounces the nunnery, marries him, and, after they've all escaped, lives happily ever after ... does this show not come equipped with all the virtues of the pre-*Show Boat* musical theatre relished by the audiences of the 1920s and before?

Back in 1943, on *Oklahoma!*'s opening night at the St. James, the stage was filled with a bright golden haze, a vista of the wide-open spaces. Onto it came a brooding villain, Jud, who threatened our pair of true lovers ... but after the dust settled, and Jud had been killed (yes, that was another broken rule, wasn't it?), we had the requisite happy ending. *Oklahoma!* filled its audience with a sense of elation and pride in the development of our new land, and it offered us a shining future, filled with hope. Whereas *The Sound of Music* would bring the curtain up on a darkly troubled Europe, and would depict characters living hemmed in by, not to mention oppressed by, Old World prescriptions of church and state — that is, until they escape from them at the finale.

More than half a century later, *Oklahoma!* still rouses us with those dazzling de Mille dances. Just think of that next-to-closing eleven o'clock number in which the cast sings "Oklahoma!," one of the most masterly stage numbers ever devised, and how it has sent audiences out of the theatre year after year with a rosy glow of what Howard Lindsay defined as "reward." Of course, he and Russel Crouse would have rewards in store for us at the end of *The Sound of Music,* too, but there would be precious little choreography — unless you regard a bunch of beaming children bobbing up and down in their bedroom, or a line of nuns gracefully moving in and out of a cathedral, or two young lovers in a delicate love duet, as anything more than simple *movement.* (Joe Layton's credit in 1959 would read "Musical Numbers Staged by ..." and for once, not even the most insistent agent would be able to contradict it.)

Like a Viennese operetta, *The Sound of Music* would have some pretty impressive scenery, Alpine and otherwise. At times the stage would be filled with Oliver Smith's settings. But did it break any rules, as Lem Ayers's design had? Not at all.

The similarity between these two remarkable musicals, at least the major one, is that both *Oklahoma!* and *The Sound of Music* are uplifting. The subtext of both contains the reward and the purge in Howard Lindsay's recipe for success. Yes, time had passed between these masterworks, and after all of Rodgers and Hammerstein's collaborative years, by the time of *The Sound of Music* they were, perhaps, no longer in the creative surprise business, as they had been back in 1943. But over the years it has never mattered. Not to any audience. The consensus is that the trip from Oklahoma to Salzburg may have been a long one, but no one minds taking it ... over and over again.

Another similarity between the two shows is that Rodgers's score was orchestrated by Robert Russell Bennett in both, and with his customary brilliance. (Of course, if you're listening for surprises in orchestrations, there's something wrong with the show, right?)

In short, the one show broke every rule of its time, and the other, nearly two decades later, abided by all of them.

THE CRAFTSMEN

Lindsay and Crouse were preparing the outline that would become the script of *The Sound of Music,* and in the following months Rodgers and Hammerstein would tackle the score. Meanwhile, producer Leland Hayward had his hands full with the details of producing that same show he'd originally offered Lindsay and Crouse, the one they'd turned down: *Gypsy.*

Hayward's coproducer, David Merrick, was clearly uninterested in *Gypsy.* Even with Ethel Merman to star as the archetypal stage mother, Rose, who drove her daughters June and Gypsy through adversity to success, Merrick couldn't whip up any enthusiasm for the project. He was far more attracted to his own venture, *Destry,* which would star Andy Griffith.

Producing *Gypsy* would not be an easy task. Hayward had struggled to bring together a cadre of highly creative talents: Jule Styne to write the music, Stephen Sondheim to pen the lyrics, Arthur Laurents to craft the book, and Jerome Robbins to choreograph and stage the production.

Hayward's days and nights were filled with a constant series of wrangles and creative arguments: director, costumer, performers, agents, lawyers all going to the mat with seemingly endless problems, artistic, emotional, and, more often than not, financial. But through it all, he persisted. He spent long hours in meetings, trying to bring *Gypsy* together, and trying to keep his fledgling production from being scuttled before it had even been launched. Such is the producer's task.

One of his friends asked him how could he put up with all these constant battles, even before there'd been a rehearsal? Why not move on to something else?

"Oh, no," he replied, "I have to stick with this one. Why so? Because it's going to be such a helluva good show."

Once *Gypsy* was open, and he'd been proven absolutely right, it was time for *The Sound of Music*.

Lindsay and Crouse had also been busy. "While they waited for Dick and Oscar, they produced a play called *Tall Story*, a comedy about basketball," recalled Mrs. Crouse. "But they also had decided they might just as well work on the book which would eventually be ready for Dick and Oscar." In other words, without conferring with Rodgers and Hammerstein. "But," she said, "they did it scene by scene, and when they'd finished one, they'd send it on to Dick and Oscar."

"It was one of the best collaborations Howard and Russel had ever had," she added. "I can give you an idea of what a good partnership it became: Early on, they wrote a scene in which the nuns are discussing Maria, and to each other they point out how she has curlers in her hair, how she whistles on the stair ... and all sorts of things about her. After Oscar read it, he called up and said 'I am going to ask you a very great favor: Would you mind if I made that into a song? It's a perfect lyric.'"

"They told him, 'Be our guest, because if you tell a story in a song, it's so much better!'"

Hammerstein proceeded to write, and from the Lindsay and Crouse scene would come:

> How do you solve a problem like Maria?
> How do you catch a cloud and pin it down?
> So many different words describe Maria—
> ... A flibbertigibbet, a will o' the wisp, a clown.

It took seventeen days to complete the lyric, which ends:

> How do you hold a moonbeam in your hand?

Truly, a master at the peak of his form.

"Oscar and Dick very kindly gave Howard and Russel part of the show album royalties in return," Mrs. Crouse remarked. "Now, that was something unheard of — for book writers to share in a cast recording. How generous of them!"

Later, the give-and-take process between Lindsay and Crouse and Hammerstein would continue, this time in reverse. When the two playwrights arrived at the scene in which Maria and Captain von Trapp come to express their mutual love, they stumbled over the problem of dialogue; none of their lines seemed to suit the situation or the characters. When they described their problem with that moment, Hammerstein would solve it for them by bringing them a lyric, "An Ordinary Couple."

Figure 2.1 A picture of collaboration: Mary Martin, flanked by Rodgers and Hammerstein on the left, and Lindsay and Crouse on the right, posed for the press photographers in 1959. (Courtesy of the Rodgers and Hammerstein Organization)

By March of 1959, the work had progressed with a remarkable shortage of problems. It was quite a different history from what usually takes place in the creation of a Broadway-bound musical.

Hammerstein took the sixty-page treatment that Lindsay and Crouse had completed and went to Jamaica to work on the lyrics at a pleasant enclave of houses called Round Hill. There was general agreement among the four on what songs were needed and where they should go in the script.

Since it was a show for which Hammerstein had not been called upon to write the book (a task that he would confide to his son James he'd have given up years before, had he only been able to find others capable of doing it for him), his days passed pleasantly, and he accomplished a great deal. While other guests lounged on the beach, he soon completed the lyrics for Maria's opening number, "The Sound of Music."

Of course, Hammerstein labored long and hard over each lyric. He kept meticulous worksheets of each day's work. Day after day, the lyrics developed slowly, almost painfully. His name for that work was "woodshedding." Hour after hour, he would remain at work, agonizing as he always had over the choice of the exact word, the perfect choice for the thought he wished to communicate.

He returned to Doylestown, still working steadily. Standing at his desk each day, as he had done all those years, he completed "My Favorite Things."

One afternoon, his son William came to visit. The two ended up in the swimming pool, where Hammerstein told Bill the story of the new show he was working on. When he'd finished, the son was in tears.

Then Hammerstein said, "I'm planning to write a song like 'You'll Never Walk Alone.'" He'd been thinking about it for some time. The lyric would emerge from his correspondence with Sister Gregory, the head of the drama department at Rosary College, in River Forest, Illinois. She had become a good friend of Mary Martin and Richard Halliday; Martin had asked her for advice and counsel on convent life. Over several months, she and Hammerstein would consult, by mail, on various aspects of the religious side of the script. Why did young women choose the religious life? Sister Gregory responded: "Everyone must find one's own answer to the simple question, What does God want me to do with my life? How does he wish me to spend my love?"

Hammerstein began his lyric with the title "Face Life," and then added Sister Gregory's questions onto the page. And then he wrote his own intuitive notes, in Maria's own thoughts: "You can't hide here. Don't think that these convent walls shut out problems. You have to face life wherever you are. You have to look for life, for the life you were meant to lead. Until you find it, you are not living."

Once he had begun exploring Maria's internal struggle for "Face Life" — to stay or not to stay in the convent — he wrote more notes about life, about climbing a hill, about getting to the top, "Which doesn't bring you much closer to the moon, but closer to the next hill, which you must also climb."

Under his own notes, Hammerstein added a warning to himself: "Don't let this be too obviously a philosophical number."

Eventually, "Face Life" would become "Climb Ev'ry Mountain." Hammerstein's lyric had a verse to begin with, and two stanzas, or choruses, to follow. When he brought it to Rodgers, who set the lyric to a very impressive musical line, the team decided that the two stanzas were strong enough, that they expressed enough to stand alone, without the verse. That is how the stanzas have remained ever since, moving the audience as deeply as they do.

When Sister Gregory received a manuscript copy of Hammerstein's lyric, she wrote back to Mary Martin, "It drove me to the Chapel. (Relax, chums, I'm sure it will not affect your audiences in the same way.) It made me acutely aware of how tremendously fortunate are those who find a dream that will absorb all their love, and finding it, embrace it to the end." She commented on how much she liked Rodgers's music, then continued, "However, it was the lyrics that sent me to the Chapel. Mr. Hammerstein's lyrics seem perfectly, yet effortlessly, to express what we ordinary souls feel but cannot communicate."

And she was also right about audiences. They don't go to a chapel after hearing "Climb Ev'ry Mountain," they come back to hear it again and again, year after year.

CHAPTER 3

Gains and Losses

During the summer of 1959, Hayward and Halliday were assembling the creative cadre for *The Sound of Music*. The costumes would be designed by Mainbocher and Lucinda Ballard. Oliver Smith was at work designing the scenery, and Robert Russell Bennett was orchestrating Rodgers's score.

Casting was supervised by Edwin Blum, from the production office of Rodgers and Hammerstein. Blum's formidable task was to bring in actors and actresses whom director Vincent Donehue could audition. Since the von Trapp brood ran from tots to teenagers, and had to be good singers, finding the right performers was a large order (as would be replacing them when they grew out of their age groups in the next few years). For choreography, there would be Joe Layton.

One of the most important casting tasks would be to find a leading man who could sing, to play opposite Mary Martin in the role of Captain von Trapp.

The name of Theodore Bikel was on the list of possibles. The actor–folk-singer was then in Holland, making a film. "My agents thought I would be an ideal choice to play the Captain," he remembered, "and I thought so, too. It goes without saying that almost every leading man in the New York theatre was dying to have a crack at the part, which forced my agents to work fast."

Bikel was flown in from Holland by Hayward and Halliday; he had forty-eight hours' leave from his Dutch assignment. "They also arranged for me to work with someone on a couple of songs for the audition. I had never done a musical before. The music I was used to performing was of a different genre from Broadway tunes — not exactly audition material, they

Figure 3.1 The first day of rehearsal: Richard Rodgers (far right) watches as director Vincent Donehue (at table) addresses Mary Martin (center right), Theodore Bikel (center), and the *Sound of Music* company on the stage of the Lunt-Fontanne. (Photo by Toni Frissell courtesy of Lauri Peters)

said. ... Big question: When you audition for Rodgers and Hammerstein, do you do one of their own tunes and risk running afoul of their concept? ... Even if you are brilliant, if you've shaped their music to your style, will it be seen as chutzpah, or even hubris?" he recalled thinking as he faced the audition.

Figure 3.1 (continued)

After some thought, Bikel ended up performing two Frank Loesser songs: "Luck Be a Lady" and "My Time of Day." "I also slipped in one of my folk songs, with my guitar," he said.

"I stood waiting while I dimly saw some heads bobbing in the dark auditorium. After a while, they thanked me for having come in to do this, and said they would be in touch with my agents. Well, that's that, I thought. It won't come to anything, but the trip was worthwhile, anyway."

Bikel returned to Holland, finished his role in the film, and then went off to visit family in Israel. From New York, silence. Finally, after waiting through several more days, he managed to get a call through from Israel to New York, and reached his agents. What was the resolution of the audition? Who'd been cast as the Captain?

The part, it seemed, was his!

"Mary Martin told me later that after I had done my folk song at the audition, she'd leaned forward, tapped Dick Rodgers on the shoulder, and whispered, 'We don't have to look any further, do we?'"

In the rest of the company would be Kurt Kasznar as Max Detweiler, and Marian Marlowe as Elsa Schraeder. "Ironically," said Bikel, "almost all the actors who would play Nazis or Nazi sympathizers in the second act were Jews — Michael Gorrin, and Stefan Gierasch. ...

"One night, I was waiting in the wings for my entrance after Franz, the butler, played by John Randolph, was to bring Captain von Trapp the telegram ordering him to report to the Nazi navy. ... He came across the stage and exited into the wings carrying the telegram on a silver tray. When he handed it to me, he said, 'Captain, *tsuris!*'—Yiddish for 'bad trouble.'"

The last week in August 1959, the show went into rehearsal at the Lunt-Fontanne Theatre on West 46th Street, where it would open in November. All was going well, but then ...

Early in September, Hammerstein went to his doctor for an annual physical checkup. When he'd finished, Hammerstein mentioned he'd been waking up hungry at night, and drinking milk to assuage it before going back to sleep. The watchful doctor suggested tests for an ulcer. The tests revealed that Hammerstein had cancer of the stomach. Surgery was absolutely necessary; it was suggested for two days later.

Before he left for his operation, Hammerstein came to the Lunt-Fontanne and met Mary Martin backstage. Whether or not he could express himself verbally, he had for many years always put the right words on paper. He handed his star a folded page. "Don't look at it now," he said. "Look at it later." Then he left.

When she did look at it, she found on the paper a lyric, the verse he'd written for "Climb Ev'ry Mountain," but which had not yet been used. It read:

> A bell is no bell till you ring it,
> A song is no song till you sing it.
> And love in your heart wasn't put there to stay.
> Love isn't love till you give it away.

Eventually, these words, so touching, so indicative of Hammerstein's philosophy, would end up as the verse to the reprise of "Sixteen, Going On Seventeen."

Figure 3.2 Director Vincent Donehue joins in as Mary Martin guides Kathy Dunn (kneeling) and Mary Susan Locke (at bottom) through a song rehearsal at the star's home. (Courtesy of Photofest)

Comforted by Rodgers, who had also had a bout with cancer and had survived, and who promised Martin, "We are going to work as long as we can," she treasured those lines, her gift from Oscar Hammerstein. For the rest of her career, she would sing his quatrain, in many languages, at the end of each performance, wherever she was in the world.

For her, Hammerstein was "the epitome of love for his fellow man."

Without him, the company continued rehearsing for the New Haven tryout opening. This would be the first Shubert tryout he could not attend. Hammerstein was recovering from the surgery, but the prognosis was not good. The carcinoma was large; the surgeons had removed most of his stomach. At best, Hammerstein would have six months to a year to live.

"It had all gone so well," recalled Mrs. Crouse. "Over the years I've worked on many shows, and I can't think of a happier collaboration than this one ... with the awful exception of our loss of Oscar."

CHAPTER 4

Out of Town

October 3, 1959: opening night in New Haven.

In came the Shubert ticket-holders; for weeks they'd been waiting for this one, Mary Martin starring in a new Rodgers and Hammerstein show. A sold-out house, with standees thronging the rear of the orchestra seating. Anyone who had seats for tonight was indeed fortunate.

Here were all those gamblers — the locals, intermingled with New York people, agents, and ticket brokers, and scouts from the movie company home offices, plus a delegation in from the Coast, here to check out whether there might be a movie in this show. And, of course, the press: Harold Bone of *Variety*, plus a couple of New York "column planters" — press agents who, by midnight, would get the word back, and then the buzz about this latest gilt-edged "R and H" offering would be out.

And there was also the squadron of friends, here to cheer on Mary Martin, and Halliday, Rodgers, Lindsay, Crouse. ...

As much as anybody knew, this show was about that Austrian Baroness von Trapp — ah yes, the refugee lady who'd brought her family out of Europe, established them as a group of choir singers, made them all a new life here. Not exactly a run-of-the-mill subject for a Mary Martin show, would you say?

Would it make a hit musical? By 11:20 p.m. or so, they'd have their answer.

The house lights went down, the rustle of conversation stopped. In contrast to the "Away We Go!" opening, all those years ago in 1942, a spotlight revealed a conductor in the Shubert pit, Frederick Dvonch. And now he raised a baton to lead the orchestra through the "Preludium," arranged by

Robert Russell Bennett. Up went the curtain, to reveal, onstage, a tree, and there was Mary Martin ... up in the tree?

Yes, and she was singing:

> The hills are alive,
> With the sound of music

"That song almost compensated for the fact that I never got my banister in our production," Martin wrote in her memoirs.

"In the German movie, Maria the postulant appears in her first scene sliding down a long, long banister. She is always late to her classes, always going as fast as she can, dashing madly to get places on time. So off she goes down the banister and lands with a nice clunk, right at the feet of the Mother Superior. I couldn't wait to do that. All through rehearsals, I kept asking 'Where's my banister?'

"I never got it. There were just too many sets, too many other things to think about. In our version I first appeared on a tree — on it — at the very top, gazing at the Alpine scenery and singing. ... The tree and I went forward, from the back of the stage towards the front, as the curtains opened. I was never madly comfortable. Not until I saw my friend Florence Henderson play Maria did I really understand how effective that entrance was. I had always felt like someone's version of a saint, being swept along, teetering a little, in a procession."

The New Haven audience loved it.

And from then on, they would be treated to a first act overflowing with the sound of music: "Maria," "Sixteen Going On Seventeen," "The Lonely Goatherd," "My Favorite Things," "Do-Re-Mi" — Richly varied Rodgers music, all with Hammerstein's lyrics, which for the first time in a long career he was unable to hear his audience respond to tonight.

Then came the final scene of the first act, when the Abbess is confronted by Maria, who must make a decision: to stay in the order, or to leave it and go back to the Captain, whom she's discovered she has feelings for, and to the children, whom she has also grown to love.

"Climb Ev'ry Mountain," sang Patricia Neway, her voice filling the Shubert. In the midst of the song, Maria realizes that she must abandon the religious life to respond to her emotions. She slowly removes the veil from her head as the initiation of her new life. Curtain.

In three very rare images from the Shubert Theatre in New Haven, here is *The Sound of Music* as captured during its tryout performances. (Courtesy of the Shubert Theatre, New Haven, Connecticut.)

No chorus, no dance number — but, truly, an emotional first-act finale. Certainly as powerful as the first act finale of *Gypsy*, Leland Hayward's latest, a thrilling coup de théâtre.

Figure 4.1 The Captain and Maria.

Figure 4.2 The Mother Superior (Patricia Neway) singing "Climb Ev'ry Mountain."

Figures 4.1–4.3 In three very rare images from the Shubert Theatre in New Haven, here is *The Sound of Music* as captured during its tryout performances. (Courtesy of the Shubert Theatre – New Haven Archives)

Figure 4.3 The von Trapp children are won over by their new governess.

During the intermission, the audience pushed its way up the aisle, out to the lobby, where the smokers could hold conference on the windy street. Hayward, Halliday, and assorted members of their staff prowled through the ticketholders, impassively eavesdropping on the chatter, checking out the reactions so far.

Yes, the show was a little long. Well, what difference did that make? Hadn't *My Fair Lady* shown up here running fifteen minutes too long? And what about *South Pacific*, which had kept everybody in their seats way past eleven-twenty? So if this latest "R and H" seemed to be a bit slow and heavy, why worry about that? These guys knew what they were doing. Wasn't Mary Martin terrific with these kids? How could you go wrong with kids like that? In the next act, she'd be marrying the Captain and raising the family — oh, maybe she was a little old for this part, but she was doing a marvelous job with it — wasn't she adorable? The lobby lights blinked.

Now it was time for that second act.

Hayward, Halliday, and Rodgers met for a brief conference before retiring to their seats. "So far, so good," was Hayward's guarded comment. "I get the feeling they like it."

He was right. But even he, the master showman–salesman given to bursts of hyperbole (one of the people who knew him well was fond of referring to him as "a guy who could sell you smoke"), could have no idea how future audiences would respond to *The Sound of Music* tonight and for years to follow.

The New Haven people fixed their attention on the second act. They watched and listened as the Captain, and Maria, now married, staunchly resist the onslaught of the Nazis into their beloved Austria, as they announce they will not fly the Nazi banner; and they heard how he would neither serve in Hitler's navy nor bow to the invaders. Then, their inevitable decision to leave their homeland. And the climax, as the von Trapps finish their command performance in Salzburg, singing "So Long, Farewell" to their compatriots.

And then, for the final scene, the family bravely scaling the mountains en route to Switzerland (not precisely true, but much more dramatic than the fact of their departure), singing "Climb Ev'ry Mountain."

And when the curtain fell, the thunder of applause. "Who could resist those ingredients?" remarked Bikel. "Seven adorable children, a chorus of gorgeous nuns' voices, and a young woman who had almost renounced any chance for a normal life."

Grateful at having been midwives at the birth of what promised to be a success, an event which in years to come they could boast about to their own children, the New Haven theatergoers went home.

The next day, the New Haven reviews were favorable — with one notable exception. The show got its first pasting, one of the many it would earn from the venerable *Yale Daily News*, where there appeared a review by Leslie Epstein. The headline read, "oh sister! mit schlage!" and beneath that irreverent salvo was "I'm Getting into the Habit with You."

Years later, Epstein recalled that Richard Rodgers was so annoyed by the *Yale Daily News* pan that when he later encountered the young critic's mother at a Hollywood social event, he told her, "Your son doesn't know his ass from his elbow!"

With some justifiable wonder, Epstein said, "He took it as a personal insult!" But, he added, "When I came to the end of my bad review, I was savvy enough, even then, to append this prediction: 'In spite of all I've said, this show is going to make a billion dollars.'" (Such prescience had to come from the Epstein gene pool: Leslie had grown up in a show-business metier, the son of Philip Epstein and the nephew of Julius, two icons of Hollywood screenwriting.)

Everyone involved in *The Sound of Music* knew full well that no matter how much the audience and the critics praised the show, there was work to do. "No one in the theatre ever takes success for granted," commented Bikel. "Too often theatre people have allowed themselves to be lulled by the early approbation of audiences so grateful for the chance at seeing a new work that they refuse to be critical."

Not such old pros as Lindsay and Crouse or Martin or Donehue or Rodgers. The October 13 opening in Boston was just around the corner, and "there was chopping and changing scenes, a constant quest, if not for perfection, then at least for the promise of it," said Bikel. "Donehue and Joe Layton did the arranging and the rearranging. But Dick Rodgers was also very much in evidence during the process of whipping the show into shape." Hammerstein, having undergone his surgery, did not arrive in Boston to rejoin the show until it was in its second week of the run.

By that time, the Boston reviews were in. Eliot Norton, the respected dean of the critics, hadn't cared for the show very much; his *Boston Herald* Sunday review would be another early example of a long line of negative notices:

> Musically, this is one of the grandest of Broadway shows; dramatically, it is weak.

> In the songs they have written for Mary Martin, for Patricia Neway, for seven singing wunderkind and for a chorus of women who have undoubtedly come down from heaven to personate nuns, Richard Rodgers and Oscar Hammerstein have matched their best work. Their music is not only melodious, it is exultant; it runs through the show in little freshets of melody, or in great tumbling rivers of sound. ... The sound of music is rich and fresh and magnificent in *The Sound of Music*. ...

> The libretto should have been equally wonderful ... for the true story of Maria Reiner is just that, and Howard Lindsay and Russel Crouse have all the qualities needed to make it move and amuse any audience. ... But they have falsified the character of the Baron so that he is presented first as a ridiculously stern parent, who makes his small children march like little storm troopers and summons his help and everyone else with a bosun's whistle. He later rebels against the Nazis — as Captain von Trapp did in real life — you are apt to wonder why. For in his own home, in those early scenes, he seems the very model of a heel-clicking, heiling tyrant.

> The Baron comes off badly in the play, and so do most of the other characters, except when *The Sound of Music* is occupied in singing one or another of the gay and great songs which roll over the play at regular intervals, inundating it in melody and in beauty. ...

> Some of the silliness, the stiffness and the corny operetta falseness of this script can be eliminated. The truth can set *The Sound of Music* free of clichés, and lift it up to that high level of excitement where the

best of it now shines and warms the hearts of the luckier playgoers of Boston. [October 18, 1959]

(Years later, Hayward was sitting at his office desk, which was covered with checks he was endorsing — a distribution of profits for the investors in *The Sound of Music*. Yet another million profit. "This has been going on for a long time," he chuckled. "Not bad for a show which the critics hated, ah?")

Hammerstein went to see the show. It was the first time in his long career that he hadn't been able to be an active participant in the preparation and day-to-day production of one of his works. There was *The Sound of Music*, spread out on a stage, playing to a full house.

"I remember he sat in a box, with his wife Dorothy," said Anna Crouse, "and Dorothy came out during the intermission to Russel, and she said, 'I have only seen Oscar' — Poppy, she called him — 'cry once in my whole married life . . . and he's been crying.' Broke your heart."

When the performance ended, the Hammersteins went backstage to talk to the assembled company. Everyone knew of his operation; most of them knew it hadn't been totally successful. Hammerstein had his notes for them. He spoke to each member of the cast, giving them his comments. If, after forty-four shows in a long career, this one was to be his last, there would be no slackening of his professionalism.

As her Poppy went through his critiques, it was Dorothy's turn to stand behind a piece of scenery backstage, and to cry.

Hammerstein did the only other thing he knew how to do. He went to work. "With eleven days to go, we thought there could be no major additions or deletions," recalled Bikel. Rodgers and Hammerstein had decided there was something lacking in the score, and it had to do with the character I portrayed. They argued that my 'special talents' had not been fully used in the show, and that my folk background and my guitar playing could be used to better advantage."

What Hammerstein, with his remarkable acuity, was seeking was a lyric that would express the sadness in the family's departure from Austria, facing an enforced exile. He came up with the idea of what would be "Edelweiss," and for the next six days, he worked on a lyric, jotting down notes, writing phrases, seeking to express the sentiment of their loss.

One of the phrases he would set down early on was certainly the subtext of Hammerstein's own frame of mind. Sadly, he had written:

Look for your lover and hold him tight
While your health you're keeping.

Figure 4.4 Theodore Bikel with Marion Marlowe, as Elsa Schraeder, and Kurt Kasznar, as Max Detweiler. (Courtesy of Photofest)

"Edelweiss" was Oscar Hammerstein's last lyric. Simply, he described a mountain flower, and by doing so, he created a remarkably strong sense of authenticity, of deep patriotism.

A piano was brought into a private room at the Ritz-Carlton, where he and Rodgers could finish the song. Then they gave it to Bikel to sing near the closing of the second act. With the actor's first performance of it, the audience response was immediate. Simple, quiet, loving, Hammerstein's swan song proved absolutely necessary for the show, as it has been ever since.

Remarkably enough, "Edelweiss" created its own aura. People automatically assumed it was a traditional Austrian folk ballad. "I sang and played it eight times a week for the next two years," said Bikel. "This beautiful little tune sounded so authentic that one autograph-seeking fan at the stage door some months later said to me: 'I love that "Edelweiss"' — and then added, with total confidence: 'Of course, I have known it for a long time, but only in German.'"

CHAPTER 5

The Sound of Applause

The New York opening would be on November 16, 1959.

By that night, there was a massive advance sale already "wrapped" — the theatrical term for tickets bought and paid for — almost two million dollars' worth of seats reserved by expectant theatregoers who wanted to see Mary Martin in whatever Rodgers and Hammerstein had created for her.

Such a large sum of faith-money was almost enough to ensure that Martin and her partners would recoup their original investment. The production's budget had been originally set at $400,000, and so shrewdly had the management put the show together that its final cost was only $20,000 over budget.

"That overage was the cost of a replacement sofa in Captain von Trapp's living room," said Frank Goodman, the production press agent. "Dick Rodgers didn't like the original one, and he insisted it be replaced."

That November night arrived, and so did the opening-night audience; into the Lunt-Fontanne they flocked. "There was incredible tension in the cast before the curtain rose," remembered Bikel. "I shared in the excitement, but felt none of the fear that seemed to grip the other cast members, including the children and the chorus. Everyone had gotten flowers, telegrams, and presents. I received a solid gold whistle as a tribute to my bosun's whistling onstage. Mary gave me a silver-framed photograph in which she wore the dress from our wedding scene. ... I gave gifts and went around the dressing rooms trying to calm everyone down. ... Then we opened."

Years later, Mary Martin remarked, "I knew that my part required perfect pitch — and I'm not talking about music now. The treatment had to be very skillful, totally controlled. It was one of the most disciplined shows I ever did. You could never do a kidding thing, never play it broadly. I had to remember the character always, keep a tight rein on my emotions and my performance."

She would certainly do so that night. The audience loved her; they were enraptured with her, with the von Trapp children, with her romance with the Captain, and with the triumphant second act closing. And, as Rodgers and Hammerstein had predicted, they were deeply moved by "Edelweiss."

The cast received a standing ovation.

"We'd gone to Sardi's for the after-theatre party," remembered Anna Crouse, "and we got to the room where the party was being held, and we were all enjoying ourselves until the word got out: Both major reviews were absolutely terrible. ... And there we all were, trying to be up and gay and cheerful, knowing that the show had been damned."

Soon enough, the early editions of the next day's papers hit the newsstands, and the reviews were there to be read.

Walter Kerr of the *Herald Tribune* said:

> I only wish that someone had not been moved to abandon the snowflakes and substitute cornflakes. Before *The Sound of Music* is halfway through its promising chores, it becomes not only too sweet for words but almost too sweet for music. Is it director Vincent Donehue who has made the evening suffer from little children? There are seven tots necessary to the narrative, and I am not against tots. But must they bounce into bed in their nightgowns so often, and so charmingly? Must they wear so many different picture-book skirts and fluff them so mightily, and smile so relentlessly, and give such precocious advice to their elders? The cascade of sugar is not confined to the youngsters. Miss Martin, too, must fall to her knees and fold her hands in prayer, while the breezes blow the kiddies through the window. She must always enter as though the dessert was here, now. The pitch is too strong; the taste of vanilla overwhelms the solid chocolate; the people onstage have all melted before our hearts do.

If Kerr had had himself a bad night, he was not alone. Brooks Atkinson, the most powerful of the New York critics, wrote in the *Times*:

> Although Miss Martin has longer hair than she had in *South Pacific*, she still has the same common touch that wins friends and influences people, the same sharp features, good will and glowing personality that makes music sound intimate and familiar. ... Mr. Rodgers has not written with such freshness of style since *The King and I*. Mr. Hammerstein has contributed lyrics that also have the sentiment and dexterity of his best work. But the scenario of *The Sound of Music* has the hackneyed look of the musical theatre they replaced

with *Oklahoma!,* in 1943 [sic]. ... It is disappointing to see the American musical stage succumbing to the clichés of operetta. The revolution of the Forties and Fifties has lost its fire.

The other critics were less captious and negative. Richard Watts, Jr., of the *Post,* wrote: "The new Rodgers and Hammerstein show has a warm-hearted, unashamedly sentimental and strangely gentle charm that is wonderfully endearing." And John McClain, of the *Journal-American,* remarked "The most mature product of the team and it seemed to me to be the full ripening of these two extraordinary talents."

But it was perhaps left to Whitney Bolton, of the *Morning Telegraph,* to make the most sagacious remark: "With better than two million dollars sacked up in the tills," he commented, "... it couldn't matter less what a critic might think."

It did, however, matter a great deal to those who'd worked so long and hard to bring Mary Martin's *What-if* to full-scale life on the Lunt-Fontanne stage. The Hammersteins went home; for Oscar and his wife Dorothy those reviews were especially depressing. "They went with Herb Mayes and his wife," remembered Mrs. Crouse. "The Mayeses lived up above the Hammersteins; they shared an elevator up to the apartments. Herb told me later that, as they were going up in the elevator, they heard Oscar give a heartfelt sigh of despair. 'It just broke my heart,' he told me later.

"Here was Oscar, who'd been through so damn much in this past summer. ... It was a real shock to all of us — to all four of the men who'd created the show. But for Oscar, it was worse. He'd come to see the show in Boston, and sat with the audiences loving it, and then that negative review from Eliot Norton. ... Perhaps he could have shrugged that one off, but here were the two most important critics in New York — Atkinson and Kerr — and they'd both given us bad reviews. Too much."

But the following night, everyone was back at the Lunt-Fontanne.

In came the audience, down went the lights, and, the "Preludium" concluded, up went the curtain. There was Mary Martin in the tree, and from the moment she began to sing "The Sound of Music," there was electricity in the theatre. The second-night audience responded with laughter, with applause, with total empathy.

"It was remarkable," said Mrs. Crouse. "We all went out into the lobby during the intermission, and Oscar came over to us. 'Make no mistake about it,' he told us. 'This is a hit!'

"And we looked at him. 'Do you really think so?'

"'Just look and listen to that audience!' he insisted. 'They couldn't care less about the reviews. I promise you, this is a *smash* hit!' And by the time the second act curtain came down, we knew he was right," she said.

Figure 5.1 Stagehands hanging the show: The Lunt-Fontanne Theatre being readied for the Broadway opening of *The Sound of Music*. (Photo by Toni Frissell courtesy of Lauri Peters)

Figure 5.2 Lauri Peters, as Leisl, with Mary Martin. (Courtesy of Lauri Peters)

Figure 5.3 Lauri Peters, as Leisl, and Brian Davies, as Rolf Gruber, her romantic interest. (Courtesy of Lauri Peters)

It wasn't hyperbole, or Hammerstein doing his best to bring himself out of depression. It was a master's innate perception of what an audience wanted.

The box-office response was healthy. There were lines each day at the Lunt-Fontanne, but in those first few days of the Broadway run, nobody, not even such a dedicated optimist as Hammerstein, could dare to envision the incredible success that the final Rodgers and Hammerstein collaboration would become. "They came in droves," Mary Martin remembered, years later. "I was given many gold medals during *The Sound of Music,* was blessed twice by monsignors, kissed by priests, and even received a special blessing from Pope John in Rome." And with a certain amount of personal satisfaction, she commented:

> If there ever was a triumph of audience over critics, it was *The Sound of Music.* ... From beginning to end, and all over the world — the United States, Australia, England, wherever it played — most of the critics and the intellectuals in the audience found it impossibly sweet. Some of them absolutely loathed it. But audiences loved it. No matter how critical the reviews were, they didn't keep the people out — they pulled them in. ... They kept finding a message in the show. They become quite passionate about it. People brought their children, reserved blocks of seats in advance. Some saw it over and over again; that was one reason why there was never an empty seat.

While those audiences responded with fervor eight times each week to his show, Hammerstein's physical condition did not improve. Always a pragmatist, he prepared himself for his demise.

"Oscar asked Dick to meet him at the Oak Room of the Plaza for lunch," wrote his biographer, Hugh Fordin.

He told him matter-of-factly that he knew he would die soon, that he had decided against treatments that would leave him to die in comfort but could not cure him. He discussed Dick's future and suggested he find a younger man to work with. "We discussed many things that day, two somber, middle-aged men sitting in a crowded restaurant talking unemotionally of the imminent death of one and the need for the other to keep going," Dick recalled. A man seated a few tables away came over to ask them to sign his menu. The stranger told them that he couldn't imagine why they looked so sad — they were so successful they couldn't have a worry in the world.

Ironically enough, his chance remark had been echoed in one of Hammerstein's earlier lyrics: "I Haven't Got a Worry in the World."

Hammerstein returned to Doylestown, where he could spend his declining days surrounded by family and friends. And with one final mountain to climb.

By August, the climb had ended. In tribute, on the evening of his passing all the lights of theatre marquees in midtown Manhattan were dimmed.

His works would go on, with delighted audiences applauding. But even Oscar Hammerstein, the dedicated optimist, could not have foreseen his last show's remarkable future history.

Martin stayed with *The Sound of Music* for the next two years. During that run, she would miss only one performance. The cause? "For the life of me, I can't remember what it was," she remarked later. "Something must have been sprained."

Her understudy, Renée Guarin, who'd been faithfully standing by month after month, was so excited that she'd finally been called to go on that she insisted Martin should listen in. She and the stage manager arranged to have the stage amplifiers turned up, and had the backstage telephone taken off the hook. In her backstage apartment, Martin, in bed, was able to listen to her understudy's one and only performance.

"She was just great," the star declared. "Later, she played Maria in an Australian production, stayed there for a while and married her stage manager."

Such lack of jealousy was merely one of her traits. "How do I remember Mary?" Bikel mused. "In the first instance, you have to understand that Mary Martin was first and foremost a professional with an awesome talent. She worked at her craft and she never let up, even after hundreds of performances. Working with her was a very rewarding experience."

His leading lady was refreshingly modest. "*The Sound of Music* was not a demanding show physically, except for the sheer distance I had to cover," she remembered. "The theatre was built on two stories, and we had a two-story set. My main dressing room was on the second floor of the theatre itself, but I also had a quick-change room on either side of the stage itself, in the wings. Just for fun, Richard, who loves statistics, put a pedometer on me once, and we found that I walked — ran — three miles at each performance, six miles on Wednesday and Saturdays!"

Stamina was one of her strongest suits; it had to be. But she did develop another problem. "For the first year, I was almost as blind as if all the lights had been out. I wasn't even aware of it. I knew all the children by their sizes and the color of their hair, and I knew Theo, as Captain von Trapp, by his comfortable presence and his marvelous voice. Then I became painfully aware that I always had headaches on Thursdays and Sundays. I went to a doctor, who examined me and explained that it was because I strained my eyes so much doing two performances on the matinee days."

The doctor would prescribe a simple solution: contact lenses.

"The first time I wore them was a matinee," she remembered. "I had put them in ... then came the scene in which I entered, alone, with my back to the Captain. His line, very stern, was 'What is your name?' I was supposed to say 'Maria Rainer.' That afternoon, onstage, I turned and saw Theo, really saw him — for the first time. He was so handsome, but much larger than I thought before. I blurted out 'Luise Rainer'" [a film star of the 1930s].

"*Luise Rainer?* I couldn't believe my ears. Theo couldn't believe his, either. He said, 'What?' and I got so completely out of my Austrian character that I drawled, in Texas style, 'Oh, ah mean ... Ah mean, my name is *Maria* Rainer.'"

"This little postulant nun, who is supposed to face the Captain bravely at their first meeting, was smiling all through the scene!" remembered Bikel. "In fact, she was smiling all through the first act, unaccountably. At the intermission I went to her dressing room, and I asked, 'Is anything the matter? You are giving a different performance.' Mary said, 'Why, what am I doing?' I said, 'You are *smiling*. A lot.' She said, 'I am? Oh, oh, I know why that is — contact lenses! You know something? I could see what you were doing; that was so lovely!'"

She had seen it all: the childrens' faces, the Mother Superior ... everybody. "She had never seen me before," marveled Bikel, years later. "Only a blur."

"We did it, we loved it, and we loved each other," recalled Lauri Peters, the young dancer who was selected to play Liesl, the oldest von Trapp daughter.

"I'd trained with Balanchine," she said, "but after a while, ballet becomes an expensive proposition. All those toe shoes ... and if you're not working, it can add up for your family." So Peters decided to find a job which could help her support herself; she was promptly hired to join the chorus in *Say, Darling*, an Abe Burrows-Comden and Green musical version of a novel by Richard Bissell.

From there, she had gone into *First Impressions*, and that is where Richard Rodgers saw her and suggested she audition for him. Without knowing she would be trying out for the role of Liesl, she arrived at his office. "I went determined to impress him," she said. "I was dressed to the nines."

Rodgers took one look at her, shook his head and said, "Go home, take off the lipstick, and the high heels, and come back tomorrow."

"I was so remarkably lucky," Peters said. "Not only to get a second chance, but to be part of that show for two years. It was a very, very special experience. All of us felt it, that morning when we arrived for the first rehearsal. We knew — we had to know — even someone as young as I, that these people we were going to work with were titans. All of them, Rodgers and Hammerstein, Lindsay, Crouse, our director Vinnie Donehue, and, of course, our star, Mary Martin. What an experience it was to work with such a group of total professionals, such craftsmen, all of them, who did it for the love of their work!

"Somehow, their professionalism extended itself to all of us in the cast — down to the youngest of the kids, and even their mothers. There was none of that usual stage-mother nightmare," she insisted, "with all the back-biting and competition. Those children who played the von Trapps were chosen with such care. They were loving and involved. Throughout the run, for all those two years' worth of performances, all of us were having such a good time!

"I wasn't even aware of a bad press. You see, we always relied on the audience reaction. The show was — and is — such a simple tale of good and evil; we could tell from our audience out front how they were palpably involved. Of course, there was a wholesomeness in our show, something which doesn't seem to exist in most of the current shows," she explained. "And there's that incredible score. Audiences ... leave the theatre humming the songs, and then go home and teach them to their kids. And that's going on today, isn't it?

"And there was Mary. There was such an electricity with her, an immediate accessibility. When she appeared in that tree at the opening, in the fork of those two branches, and began to sing." Peters shook her head fondly at the memory. "There she was, reaching out to them, and they immediately reached back. People got chills from that moment. And it was exactly that way, with the same reaction, for the entire two years. Every performance! ... People stop me, even now," Peters said (thirty-odd years after those first audiences saw her), "and they tell me how much they liked it, and how fondly they remember me doing 'I Am Sixteen, Going On Seventeen.' It's truly amazing!"

And what were the ex-ballerina's memories concerning the choreography?

"The dancing?" she asked. "I did all there was!"

"There is something wonderfully timeless about the show," she mused. "I guess it's because we've been through so much — and we come back to this show to get a sense of love, and good triumphing over evil — that 1950s sense that there is good, and there is love. The show presents that to you, and makes no apology for it."

Week after week, they played to sold-out houses.

Nothing seemed to faze Martin, not even the accident she had while doing the TV performance of *Peter Pan*, which she filmed in the NBC television studios in Brooklyn during days she wasn't playing matinees. She survived a schedule that would have dismayed most leading ladies, and then, one disastrous day, she slammed into an NBC studio wall and broke her arm. That night, she had to play a show. Should her understudy replace her? No, indeed; with her arm in a sling, Mary Martin went on.

In the first act of the show, it didn't matter much; her arm was folded in a sling, and since, as a postulant, her arms were meekly folded to her sides most of the time, nobody seemed to notice anything amiss. The sympathetic backstage crew had prepared slings for their star in the proper colors to match the rest of her costumes. But the true crisis came when Mary had to play the guitar. "I stuck my guitar between my sling and left side, and pretended to strum with my right hand while a musician in the orchestra pit filled in the guitar music," she remembered. Later, she performed an Austrian folk dance in the "Edelweiss" number: "Theo Bikel did his part of the dance with even more than his usual enthusiasm, waving his arms like mad, and never seemed to notice that I was waving only one arm!"

Rodgers also wrote admiringly of Martin: "Working with Mary made me appreciate even more what an extraordinary trouper she is. During rehearsals and during the run of the show on Broadway, she was constantly in training, both vocally and physically. Nothing we ever suggested was ever considered too demanding. Even after it seemed impossible to do anything with her part, Mary was still working to improve her interpretation. In all the years I've known her, I have never seen her give a performance that was anything less than the best that was in her."

From a man known for his perfectionism, high praise indeed.

There would be extraordinary examples of audience loyalty to the star and her show, such as the memorable night in July 1960, when Manhattan suffered through a power failure. Shortly before curtain time, all the lights on Broadway and its environs went out.

But the audience for that night's performance of *The Sound of Music* had no intention of leaving. They stood quietly under the darkened Lunt-Fontanne marquee, holding their precious tickets, waiting for the theatre doors to open. The theatre managers came out to inform the people that there were no lights inside. There could be no show; musicians couldn't read music in the dark, scenery could not be moved without power, nobody could perform on a darkened stage.

Still, nobody moved.

"They had come to see *The Sound of Music,* and they were going to stay there until they saw it," remembered Mary Martin. Power or not. This proved to be an extreme case of that old showbiz adage "The show must go on." Halliday quickly sent stagehands out to buy flashlights, as many as could be found. While they were out scouting for the hundred or so they returned with, Halliday consulted with the musicians and the rest of the backstage crew. "They caught the spirit," Martin said, "... and they said they'd do their best. And away we went!"

The theatre doors were opened, by flashlight. Then the ushers, with flashlights, led the audience inside. When they were seated, the star came onstage and explained the problem. "And I told them we'd carry on if they wanted us to. They did!"

What transpired then certainly deserves a place in the *Guinness Book of Records,* as one of the most amazing theatrical performances ever recorded: a full-scale Broadway musical being done by a cast by flashlight on a bare stage. Mary Martin recalled:

I sang my opening number wearing my dressing gown, and sitting on a stepladder, instead of up in the tree — and I held a flashlight to

Figure 5.4 Mary Martin teaches "Do-Re-Mi" to the youngsters in the cast. (Top:) Lauri Peters (Liesl); (second row:) William Snowden (Friedrich), Kathy Dunn (Louisa), Joseph Stewart (Kurt); (bottom:) Marilyn Rogers (Brigitta), Mary Susan Locke (Marta), Evanna Lien (Gretl). (Courtesy of the Shubert Theatre — New Haven Archives)

my face. Those darling children, in the wings, were watching me do it, and when they came on, they too held flashlights to their faces so the audience could see them, see their mouths, and understand their lyrics better.

We had no time to rehearse what we were going to do; those children simply watched me, and every single one, so quickly, did the same thing. What pros they were!

The audience in the dark theatre gave the cast a roaring round of applause — "the sound of music to our ears!" she said proudly.

Half an hour into the performance — *click* — the lights abruptly came back on again!

"We must have looked pretty funny up there, in our dressing gowns or street clothes. ... We stopped, everything stopped," Martin remembered, "and I walked down to the footlights and asked if they would like to wait a few minutes while we put on costumes and set the stage." The audience agreed enthusiastically. So, back went the cast to their dressing rooms to get into their costumes; the stagehands went to work setting up the scenery; and then, sans makeup, the cast returned to the stage to pick up where they'd left off — now in a regular performance.

When the curtain finally fell, there were cheers, and calls for encores!

"But I think it was almost a letdown," commented Mary Martin, a bit ruefully. "I think they'd probably rather have watched us finish up the entire show by flashlight. ... That audience had never experienced anything like it; that night, they felt as if they were part of the show."

Finally, the star's two-year run was almost over; eight times a week she'd enchanted the audiences. Meanwhile, the producers had cast the touring company, which would star Florence Henderson as Maria von Trapp.

"I remember that the night before the company left New York to open in Detroit was a Sunday," said Anna Crouse. "So it was decided to use the Lunt-Fontanne sets to do a run-through, and they invited a preview audience, including Mary, who, of course, had never seen the show from the front of the house. And at the intermission, we couldn't find Mary. She was down on all fours, feeling around the floor where she'd been sitting. Russel said, 'Mary, what is the matter?' And she said, 'I've cried my lens out.'

"Isn't that wonderful? Because she'd been playing it night after night, and she never knew what the effect was on the audience."

Figure 5.5 Maria weds the Captain at Nonnberg Abbey surrounded by familiar faces and a set designed in the grand tradition by Oliver Smith. (Courtesy of Photofest)

CHAPTER 6

The Passing of the Torch

The Sound of Music would eventually run for 1,433 performances. When it finally closed, it had been almost five years since the day when Mary Martin had first been approached by Vincent Donehue to suggest the idea of her playing Maria von Trapp. Five years since she and Dick Halliday had borrowed enough money to buy the rights to the German Trapp Family films and start the project. Five years since all the rest of that remarkably creative group, Leland Hayward, Howard Lindsay and Russel Crouse, Richard Rodgers and the dear, departed Oscar Hammerstein, had joined her and Halliday and Donehue to make the whole thing happen to create a classic American musical — one that withstands all sorts of bad reviews.

"Mary and I left the show on the same day, two years in the Lunt-Fontanne and one month on the road after we'd started," said Theodore Bikel. "I had wanted out earlier, or at least to be sprung for a film job with a promise to return to the show. No dice. For all our friendship, Mary insisted that I stay with the play. She hated change of any kind.

"But in some cases, change could not be helped. For example, some of the children had to be let go because of the difference in their growth rates. The idea was that when standing in line, they should look like organ-pipes, in an ascending or descending order. ... Some of the kids simply grew too fast, and two of the children suddenly would be the same height. The faster-growing kid had to be replaced."

And that was not all. "Mary was used not only to their height, but also to the color of their hair. When she sang 'Do-Re-Mi,' she tapped the kids' heads for different notes. Once they replaced a blonde-haired child with a dark-haired one, and Mary insisted that they dye the new child's hair the exact color as the old one's, so she wouldn't get mixed up!

"After two years," concluded Bikel, "both Mary and I were quite prepared to say goodbye ... but when the actual night came, it was a surprisingly difficult thing for all of us to face. There were places in the performance that had us all choked up and almost unable to continue. The children singing 'So Long, Farewell,' which we had heard so often, suddenly took on a personal meaning and touched us, not as the Captain and Maria, but as Mary and Theo."

The end of their last performance arrived. "After the final curtain, Mary and I stood onstage amid grown-ups and children, all with tears in their eyes, and we did not want to leave. Finally, Mary's dresser pulled her away. I stayed and shook hands, hugged stagehands, nuns, and children. Then I left to take off my makeup and clear out my dressing room, which would be occupied on Monday by a stranger.

"On the next Sunday," he said, "I was all right — that had been my day off all along — but on the Monday, I was frantic, and could not bear to be in New York. I went to spend the day with friends in Poughkeepsie, but even there, when seven-thirty rolled around, the time for the half-hour call, I was itching all over. This is what a junkie feels like, I thought, when he needs his fix!"

Bikel was far from alone in recalling such a conditioned reflex. Thousands of others have been affected by *The Sound of Music* over the last few decades in similar fashion.

SOGGY NOTICES

Given the success of the show, what about those bad reviews?

Kenneth Tynan, in his review for *The New Yorker*, had sniffed, "For children of all ages, from 6 to 11. ... The book is damp and dowdy, like a remaindered novelette."

Audiences didn't seem to agree. The touring company went out on the road for two and a half years, and when it closed in November 1963, it had played a total of thirty-five cities.

"Instead of offsetting sweetness with lightness, it turns sticky with sweetness and light," wrote Louis Kronenberger in *Time*. "[It] ends by making its warmheartedness as cloying as a lollipop, as trying as a lisp."

That was not the opinion of the show's press agent, Frank Goodman. "They gave me a small piece of the show out of friendship," he said of Hayward, Halliday, Rodgers, and Hammerstein. "My share was worth $1,000. For years I've been getting checks. I think by now my share adds up to about $25,000 or more."

In 1961 *The Sound of Music* opened in London, at the large Palace The-atre. In England, recalled Anna Crouse, the performing company was truly not a good one: "In those days," she explained, "the British laws wouldn't permit you to have children on a stage — some old regulation against the exploitation of under-agers. And so we had to have gnomes playing the children of the von Trapps — midgets! Which was awful!

"We went to the opening night, and then Russel and I went back to Claridge's. We were in a little back room — I think they'd cleaned out some maid's room, or something, but it was fine. We had a lovely room waiter who brought us breakfast after the opening night, and we sat there and read the notices":

> Only Rodgers' almost infallible ear for a tune saves the evening from foundering in a marsh of treacle, bathed in a dim religious light. [Bernard Levin, *Express*]

> It is a mistake to treat the von Trapps as heroes. This falsity of feeling undermines the whole entertainment. [Harold Hobson, *Sunday Times*]

> Take the basic story of *The King and I*, scrape the oriental spicing and substitute Austrian sugar-icing an inch thick. Add a little bit of drama at the end. Serve — and sit back and listen to the praises of the flavor. [W. A. Darlington, *Daily Telegraph*]

"I have never read such notices in my life!" Mrs. Crouse exclaimed. "We're sitting there, with all the London papers knocking the show, and our waiter comes back and he says, 'Oh, congratulations! You have that mar-velous hit.'

"And Russel said, 'What?' He held up the papers. 'These?'

"And our waiter said, 'Oh, don't pay any attention to those notices!'"

Prescient waiter, indeed.

The English production would finally close in January 1967, after a remarkable run of 2,385 performances. In the special *Variety* showbiz lingo, it was celebrated as "london 'sound' longevity champ."

"We had another review in London," said Anna Crouse. "One of the critics referred to the show as a 'soggy old plum.'"

So much for the British critics.

There is an old and trusted show business saying that probably may help to explain the incredible appeal of *The Sound of Music* in the face of all the derogatory reviews it garnered over the years. (Remember, we haven't even come to the ones that awaited the motion picture version.) It's simple enough: "Nobody liked it except the people."

How is it that *The Sound of Music* goes on ticking, providing audiences with satisfaction?

"First of all," mused Theodore Bikel, decades later, "it has to be the reverence for the material by all those people who worked on the show."

"This show," said Anna Crouse, "was put together by four men who knew what they were doing. Russel and I were married twenty-one years, and I've heard him talk about his earlier shows, and I never remember anything he and Howard did that went so smoothly and happily. I don't mean they didn't argue, or change things — of course they did, but it was all created in such a professional manner."

"It's a show about individualism," said Bikel. "On the one hand, you have a young nun who breaks away from the rigidity of convent life ... and so does the Captain. He could stay behind in Austria and become a Nazi, but no, he wants his freedom. They both break free, one for love, the other for principle. They risk all sorts of dangers for themselves, and for their family, and in the end, good triumphs over evil. What could be more satisfactory?"

And not only to audiences here in America, but all over the world.

"Did you know that when the movie came out in China, it was a huge success?" he added. "The film ran and ran — they loved it! Now you tell me, what do the Chinese know from nuns, or Nazis, or Austrian noblemen?"

LEHMAN AND LAZAR

Any Rodgers and Hammerstein opening night was certain to draw an in-crowd, those socialites and business people, movers and shakers from uptown and downtown — and from Hollywood. That November night in 1959 when *The Sound of Music* opened, down front in a pair of the best seats were two very important audience members sitting and watching the musical version of Maria von Trapp's saga.

One of them was Spyros Skouras, the head of Twentieth Century-Fox. His company had been a comfortable partner with Rodgers and Hammerstein over the years since they had agreed to work on *State Fair* back in 1945. In the mid-1950s three of Rodgers and Hammerstein's major musicals, *South Pacific*, *Carousel*, and *The King and I*, had been made into successful Fox films. When Fox had made the deal for *The King and I*, the studio secured the right of "first refusal" on any forthcoming Rodgers and Hammerstein musical.

Next to Skouras sat Irving "Swifty" Lazar, the archetypal agent, who'd built his career by specializing in selling the highest-quality merchandise to the highest-quality purchasers at, needless to add, the highest prices. In matters of quality, Lazar was the lineal heir to Leland Hayward. Tonight he represented not only Hayward but also Lindsay and Crouse and Rodgers and Hammerstein.

According to the legend, on this opening night, while the von Trapp story unfolded, Skouras could be seen weeping at what he saw and heard. When Lazar took notice of the old titan's reaction, the sight of Skouras giving way to his emotions told him everything he needed to know: He had hooked himself a "live one."

But not quite yet. Lazar knew that Fox had not exercised its right of first refusal on buying the rights to *Flower Drum Song*. That show had been sold to Universal. And since the New York reviews of *The Sound of Music* weren't written yet, who could be certain that Skouras would dip into Fox's diminishing supply of cash to pay the very high price Lazar was preparing to ask?

It would be a while before the deal was struck, especially after the two most important New York critics, Brooks Atkinson and Walter Kerr, proved — as we can now recall — to be no big fans of *The Sound of Music*.

Two weeks after that opening night, the very talented screenwriter Ernest Lehman came to New York on assignment. At the end of a day's work, he took his wife to see *The Sound of Music*. Lehman, an ex–Broadway press agent who had turned his experiences in that exotic trade into the classic screenplay *The Sweet Smell of Success*, had followed it with a string of impressive screenplays — for *Sabrina*, then the Alfred Hitchcock thriller *North by Northwest*, *From the Terrace*, and *The King and I*. He'd worked closely with Robert Wise, who had directed Lehman's script of *Executive Suite*, as well as his *Somebody Up There Likes Me*. And now he was at work on Wise's production of *West Side Story*.

During the intermission of *The Sound of Music*, Lehman remembers racing with his wife to the nearby Howard Johnson's for a bowl of chowder. There he told her: "I know the critics have beaten this show around the head, but I don't care what they say; someday this show is going to make a very successful movie." It would be several years before Lehman's prediction could begin to come true, but how could he have foreseen that, when it did, he himself would be one of the linchpins in the successful production of a classic musical movie? Before he left New York, Lehman repeated his opinion to David Brown, one of the key Fox executives in Manhattan, and then, back in Hollywood, he gave his enthusiastic recommendation to Buddy Adler, then the president of Twentieth Century-Fox.

By that time, the weekly box-office grosses were being reported by *Variety*; the word was out: *The Sound of Music* was a hot ticket, very definitely a commercial success. So, by the following June, in 1960, the persistent Swifty Lazar had closed the deal with Fox. The studio exercised its right of first refusal and bought the screen rights. The price? One and a quarter million dollars, against 10 percent of the gross. (Pay attention to that innocent-seeming word "gross," please. We did not say "net," which translates as an invisible profit, never seen in the film business. No, Lazar had negotiated 10 percent of what is known in the film business as "the first dollar," that is, the audience's cash collected at the ticket window.)

It would be the largest sum paid for a property by a film studio until that time.

Anna Crouse vividly recalled those negotiations, as well she might: "Swifty sat and explained to Howard and Russel, 'I have gotten them to put a clause in this contract which stipulates that you'll also get a percentage after the film has made $12 million.' Howard said, 'Swifty, that's just wasting ink. Nothing has ever made $12 million profit.'

"Well, of course, Howard was right — in the 1960s, no film had ever earned that much," Mrs. Crouse declared. Thirty-odd years after the release of the film, she added fervently. "All I can say today is, thank God for Swifty!"

Part of the deal Lazar negotiated also stipulated that Twentieth Century-Fox would control the rights to the original two German films about the von Trapps for a period of six years. Fox would combine the two films into one and have them dubbed into English. They would be released in the United States a year later. Does it surprise anyone to know that the reviews in 1961 were negative? "Uncompromisingly sentimental nature has a tendency to slop over into naiveté," said the *Variety* critic.

CHAPTER *7*

The Filmmakers

The Twentieth Century-Fox agreement with *The Sound of Music* partnership stipulated that no film of the musical could be released before December 31, 1964, or until all first-class presentations of the musical had closed, whichever came first. So, for the next three years, the Fox accounting department would issue six-figure checks, in installments, to maintain the studio's rights. Unfortunately, that same Fox accounting department was faced with dwindling revenues.

Darryl F. Zanuck, the powerful head of the studio's production, had decamped from Hollywood in 1956 to set himself up as an independent producer in Paris. Control of the company passed to Spyros Skouras, in New York. The studio would be run by a series of executives, with varying results, in a downward spiral of fading success.

The movie business was far from what it had been during its glory years. That twelve-inch TV screen in our living rooms, which heretofore had seemed only an interesting toy, had grown into an all-pervasive monster. Executives who'd shrugged off the video screen as trivia soon to pass found the TV networks treading more and more on their Achilles' heel, the audience.

Then came *l'affaire Cleopatra*.

It didn't begin as one of the largest projects Fox had ever attempted. Like Topsy, it just grew. And grew, and grew — until the film, which starred Elizabeth Taylor, Richard Burton, and Rex Harrison, became a cash-eating monster. By the time that barge had floated down the Nile to completion, it would almost sink the entire studio beneath its weight of nearly $40 million in costs.

57

A shrewd observer of the motion picture scene once remarked, "The Hollywood studios are just like someone who tries to commit suicide in public, but never quite succeeds." In order to find the money to pay for the Italian production costs incurred by *Cleopatra,* Skouras sold off the studio's vast back lot, a choice tract of 260 acres. It eventually became the great urban sprawl of buildings, hotels, theatres, and malls known as Century City.

But the losses continued to mount, and the various heads of production whom Skouras had installed to replace Zanuck weren't savvy enough to bring forth box-office winners.

Fox reissued all its previous Rodgers and Hammerstein film versions, *Carousel, South Pacific,* and *The King and I,* in an effort to generate cash. But in the face of the problems incurred by the behemoth *Cleopatra,* who could contemplate investing money in a film based on *The Sound of Music*?

Eventually, in what must be compared with a cliché climactic ride to the rescue, Zanuck returned from Paris, bringing with him his film *The Longest Day,* a blockbuster packed with stars reenacting the events of D-Day, in 1944. The film would bring in desperately needed grosses. But before he handed it over to Fox, Zanuck took over the reins of the company again. After all, he was the major stockholder, and he wasn't about to permit the company to go under. He'd gambled with *The Longest Day.* His gamble paid off.

Before Zanuck returned to Paris, he installed his son and heir, Richard Zanuck, as head of the daily operation of the Westwood studio, with orders to bring the company back from the brink.

Pictures were still in the Fox pipeline. Director Robert Wise was to go to Asia to make *The Sand Pebbles,* and in England and Italy, Zanuck had arranged for *Those Magnificent Men in Their Flying Machines,* as well as *The Agony and the Ecstasy.* But the once-thriving Westwood lot was almost dormant. It was time for desperate measures; young Zanuck was forced to lay off most of the personnel and to shut down the plant temporarily while he planned its future. The place became a near ghost town. Even the commissary had to shut down, while Zanuck searched for a prospective lifesaver.

What would make a blockbuster for the future?

Down in the story department files, gathering dust in the empty offices, there was a manuscript by Howard Lindsay and Russel Crouse, set to the music of Richard Rodgers and the lyrics of Oscar Hammerstein. A manuscript of a show that was still packing in audiences, now at the Mark Hellinger Theatre in New York. Why hadn't anyone in the Fox studio thought of having a film script prepared of the property Lazar had sold them?

"Even though we couldn't release the picture until the show had closed," commented young Zanuck, "they could have put a writer on it. What you want to do is have your movie ready for release when your date comes."

And what writer could that be? One who'd already gone on record with his opinion of the show as a potential hit film, Ernest Lehman, who'd recently been working with Robert Wise on the screenplay for *West Side Story*, and was completing another major film at MGM, *The Prize*. Was he still enthusiastic about writing a screenplay? He was, and he would.

Very shortly, the *Variety* headline read: "Sound" of 20th Prod'n Heard; Lehman Inked. Lehman arrived at the sprawling, empty Fox studio to meet with his new employer. Zanuck had chosen a small bungalow as his headquarters — no lavish suite for him, unlike his father. Where to house Lehman? The studio manager, one of the few employees left, told him, "You can have any office in the place." He then took Lehman on a guided tour of deserted office spaces. There was first the studio chief's suite — no phones ringing, forsaken desks, silence. The suite assigned to the story department head? Also vacant. A series of producers' suites, all available. Which one did Lehman fancy?

"It was the same as that old story: A guy calls up the movie theatre to ask, 'What time does the movie go on?' and the manager says, 'What time can you get here?'" observed Lehman. Eventually, he settled for a small office in the production department, there to begin the task of adapting *The Sound of Music* into a future Fox film that had yet to be approved by the board of directors, but that was desperately needed to bring life back to the dormant studio. Each morning, Lehman would arrive at his quiet quarters after a walk down studio streets where rows of empty parking spaces were mute evidence that no one was working on the nearby sound stages. Then on into the production building, its hallways once filled each day with Zanuck's busy staff of technicians, messengers, film crews, actors hurrying to meetings, agents hustling jobs at the casting department for their clients, cadres of assistants busily working out costs in endless production meetings ... now all of them had vanished, dissolved, faded to black. Where were they? Sitting hopefully at home, on unemployment insurance, waiting for a phone call that could bring a welcome summons back to work.

Not for nothing is Hollywood known as the dream factory.

How could they know that their future was now in the two hands of a single talented screenwriter, seated in an office with a secretary to do his typing? It was almost a surrealist image, dreamed up by someone like a Luis Buñuel or Federico Fellini: an entire studio, once mighty and thriving, now teetering on the edge of the cliff, below which waited bankruptcy. Its

future totally dependent on one writer, a lone producer ... a small but determined team, using each hour to try and snatch Fox back from the brink.

A true, traditional ninth-reel climax, with precisely the sort of suspense
that keeps paying customers coming in to sit on the edge of their seats and
pray for a happy ending.

"Dick Zanuck and I met for our first lunch at Romanoff's, to talk about
the project," Lehman recalled. "He didn't get to our table directly because
he was accosted by Swifty Lazar. I watched them as they talked for about
five minutes, and then finally Dick shook his head, walked away from
Lazar, came over to our table and sat down.

"He said, 'You know what just happened? Lazar, on behalf of an
unnamed client, just offered me $2 million — a $750,000 profit for Fox
— if I would turn *The Sound of Music* over to him. I told him no. I said,
'That's great news. I wonder who it could be?' We speculated, but we didn't
come up with any names.

"When I got back to my office, the phone rang; it was Lazar. He said
'Ernie, what are you doing over there, working on *The Sound of Music?*
They're kidding you. They're never going to make the picture. They have
no money! You'll never even get paid!' I said, 'Irving, you just offered Dick
Zanuck a $750,000 profit, and he said no!'

"Lazar just kept right on talking."

It would be a year later before Lehman et al. could discover that the
unnamed Lazar client who'd made that offer for *The Sound of Music* was
the rival studio head Jack Warner. Did Warner wish to produce the film?
No — he had a musical project of his own in progress, *My Fair Lady*, and he
had shrewdly perceived *The Sound of Music* to be a threat to his own film!

And he would be absolutely correct.

The Fox board of directors eventually gave Zanuck the green light for
production. But the actual task of turning the Broadway musical into a
successful motion picture that could revive Twentieth Century-Fox would
prove to be a classic uphill struggle.

As is customary, most of the Hollywood colony were naysayers. In that
arena known as the movie business, if you are down, even temporarily, you
are automatically out. The game goes on without you. One day, when the
Fox commissary had reopened to serve the technicians who'd been brought
back to work on two other projects, Lehman came in for lunch. There he
met Burt Lancaster, his old friend and the star of his *The Sweet Smell of
Success.* What was Lehman currently working on? Lehman told him about
the screenplay of *The Sound of Music* that was in his typewriter. Lancaster
shook his head sadly. "Jesus," he remarked, "you must need the money."

On another evening, Lehman was a guest at Jack Lemmon's home;
another guest was Billy Wilder. When, as is traditional in Hollywood

soirees, there came the discussion of forthcoming projects, Lehman mentioned *The Sound of Music*. Wilder shook his head. "Believe me," he predicted, "no musical with swastikas in it will ever be a success!"

Another negative reaction would come from director Stanley Donen, whom Lehman had thought of as a potential coworker on the film. Donen had considerable experience in musicals at Metro-Goldwyn-Mayer; Lehman called him in Switzerland to suggest he take charge of the project. Donen's reply was totally negative. "Ernie," he said, "I'm an investor in the show, and that is enough for me. Thanks, but no thanks."

Lehman's next choice was Gene Kelly, who'd directed the New York production of *Flower Drum Song*. "I went to Gene's house in Beverly Hills," recalls Lehman, "and I pleaded with him to direct the picture. He led me out the front door, and on the front lawn he said 'Ernie, go find someone else to direct this piece of shit!'"

Then came another possibility: Bob Wise, who had done *West Side Story* with Lehman. But Wise was preparing *The Sand Pebbles* for Fox. He did not wish to abandon that project; besides, in the opinion of his agent, Wise was not particularly interested in doing *The Sound of Music*. Whether or not he'd heard all the Hollywood predictions of its failure, according to his agent Wise didn't feel it was something for him.

At least, not then. (Everyone in the movie business reserves the right to change his mind.) So Lehman continued working away at the screenplay, and the search for a director went on.

Young Zanuck hadn't yet actually seen the musical, so both men went to New York. "I hadn't seen it in two years," recalled Lehman. "Mary Martin was no longer in it; she'd been replaced by Nancy Dussault, and the night we went, I remember I sat there thinking, '*This* is what I said two years ago would someday make a successful movie? *This* is what I've agreed to do?' ... Now it's one thing to say a show would make a great movie someday, but it's another thing to know you're now committed to do it!"

The curtain fell. Lehman and Zanuck left the theatre. "Dick and I were sort of not saying much to each other as we walked out. We were in deep dismay."

The following day there would be a meeting at the summit with Darryl Zanuck, who'd arrived from France to confer on possible directors and stars.

Thus began a round of Cast-O, the game constantly played in executive suites when a film is being readied for production. Zanuck threw out the first pitch: as Maria von Trapp he suggested Doris Day. It seemed Marty Melcher, her husband, had been lobbying on the star's behalf, and Zanuck was partial to the idea of the cheerful blonde singer joining the Trapp family.

Lehman was negative about the suggestion; in his opinion, Doris Day would be typical old-fashioned Hollywood typecasting. Besides, wasn't it a bit previous to start casting this film without a director? Eventually, the conversation got around to William Wyler. Who could fault such a prospect? Wyler was an icon, capable of doing not only such romantic classics as *Wuthering Heights* but also *The Best Years of Our Lives* and *Mrs. Miniver.* And lately, he'd directed the charming romantic comedy *Roman Holiday.*

Impressive credits; yes, indeed, Wyler would be perfect. Zanuck called California, suggested the project to Wyler, and immediately arranged for the director to come east and see the show with Lehman.

"I waited in New York, Willy arrived, and I took him to see the show," said Lehman. "This was now the third time I'd seen it ... and this time I was even less sure of my original judgment."

Zanuck was waiting for the two men at "21."

"We're walking out of the theatre and Willy says, 'Ernie, I hate to tell you this, but I hated the show, and I'm not going to meet Darryl!' I said, 'You have to; he's waiting for us!'"

The car arrived at "21," but Wyler refused to get out. Lehman told the chauffeur to go inside and tell Zanuck that they would not be there to meet with him, and then suggested to Wyler they go for a walk.

"It's late at night, and he keeps saying 'Ernie, I can't tell you how much I hated the show, but please, keep telling me why you think I ought to do it.'"

Lehman and Wyler walked the Manhattan streets while Lehman explained all his plans for the projected screenplay, the character changes he proposed, and the climactic moments he'd begun to strengthen visually for the screen. As if in a litany, Wyler's response was, "I hate the show, Ernie, but keep talking. Explain to me why I ought to do it."

This roving "pitch-meeting," in which a writer tries to sell a project, continued until after 2 a.m., at which point the exhausted Lehman said, "Willy, I've got one question for you. Remember that moment where Captain von Trapp begins to sing 'The Sound of Music' with his children?"

"Funny you should mention that," said Wyler. "I almost cried."

"That's it, Willy!" said Lehman. "That's why this is going to make a very successful movie. That moment!"

"Keep talking," said Wyler.

When Lehman reported this to Darryl Zanuck the following day, to explain why Zanuck had been stood up at "21," Zanuck's immediate response was, "Okay, Ernie, your job is not to work on the screenplay. Your job is to stay with Willy Wyler and keep twisting his arm until he agrees to do the movie!"

Lehman would carry out his assignment from Zanuck for the next few weeks in California, continuing to confer with Wyler day after day.

"Willy was well known for agreeing to make a picture, and then changing his mind," said Lehman. "So I kept on offering him all my suggestions for strengthening the screenplay, and eventually, as I was about to run out of ideas, Willy said okay, and we had ourselves a director!"

At least, for the moment.

For Wyler still hated *The Sound of Music*. Lehman was far from certain the arrangement with him was a lasting commitment. "I was still very leery. All I could remember is that he had hated the show, and I'd talked him into doing it. Which was far from a firm commitment."

For the next four months, Lehman worked on "treatments," carefully plotted drafts of sequences for the screenplay, with descriptions of the action therein, and proposed dialogue. Meanwhile, he and Zanuck had hired Roger Edens, the veteran musical man-of-all-work, who'd been involved at Metro for many years working on Arthur Freed productions. Eventually, all three, Lehman, Wyler, and Edens, would fly to Austria to search for locations in and around Salzburg.

There would ensue a truly comic-opera sequence in Austria. Most of the time the trio were there, it seemed Wyler would spend much of his time accepting long-distance calls from other studios, to discuss other film projects. And since Wyler had suffered hearing loss during his service in the Air Force in World War II, he would often ask Lehman to act as his go-between. Thus Lehman became aware that Wyler was in the midst of discussing an MGM project, *The Americanization of Emily,* which was being prepared for the cameras. To top that off, the film was to star Julie Andrews, the same Julie Andrews whose name had come up as a potential Maria for *The Sound of Music*. "The same Julie Andrews," said Lehman, "whom Willy felt was wrong for Maria!"

A comic opera, perhaps, but it wasn't funny. Certainly not for Lehman, who'd been working on the project all these months, doggedly attempting to get the film ready for a possible production.

Wyler suggested Lehman join him in a flight over the Austrian Alps to seek out opening shots. Lehman refused; Wyler was adamant. Lehman dug in his heels. "I guess it wasn't just the ride I was afraid of; I don't know why I didn't want to go. I guess it was my mistrust of Willy."

Later, Lehman would realize he'd been right not to go. Roger Edens, who'd gone along on the flight, reported that they'd discovered their pilot had been a Nazi. "When Wyler discovered that, all hell broke loose!" said Lehman. "There they were flying over the Alps, screaming at each other about Nazism! Boy, was I lucky I hadn't gone along!"

One cannot totally fault Wyler for his attitude. He, of Austrian parentage, had spent the early Nazi years making films in Hollywood. Many of his relatives had not been so fortunate; they'd ended up in death camps. Even though Wyler had joined the Air Force and made the remarkable documentary *Memphis Belle,* he was still determined to reveal the evils of the Nazi regime. Later on, in his own autobiography, he would admit: "I knew the movie wasn't really a political thing, but I had a tendency to want to make it, if not an anti-Nazi movie, one which at least would say a few things."

Richard Zanuck would later remember: "Willy was going to make it very heavy-handed at the end. He wanted tanks, he wanted the Germans marching into Austria, blowing up the town, a true militaristic climax." That is, a vision opposed to Lehman's adaptation of the original Lindsay and Crouse script.

Once the trio returned to California, Zanuck and Lehman went into conference. Lehman said he was concerned about Wyler's attitude. It wasn't about Wyler's method of arguing, debating, questioning, scene after scene. "I knew he ate writers alive," said Lehman. "It was that same bull-dog tenacity which indicated Willy's true attitude towards a project. The tougher he was on a script, the more he really respected it." No, what was making Lehman nervous were the stacks of books in Wyler's office; they all seemed to deal with the Anschluss, Hitler's annexation of Austria. And then there were the endless phone calls from MGM, involving the imminent production of *The Americanization of Emily*.

In the interim, the long-awaited monster production of *Cleopatra*, in which most of Fox's capital was invested, had sailed into theatres, and wonder of wonders, it was doing business! In fact, so many ticketbuyers had shown up to put down cash and sit through the mammoth spectacle that they were providing a welcome infusion of capital into the depleted Fox bank accounts. Once again, suicide had been avoided.

There was so much gross coming in that the company would now be able to bankroll *The Agony and the Ecstasy, Those Magnificent Men in Their Flying Machines*, and, last but far from least, *The Sound of Music*.

Lehman's first-draft screenplay proved to be, substantially, the finished version. "Dick had told me, 'We've got to smoke Willy out. You've got to write a first draft, very fast,'" said Lehman. "I told him 'I can't write a screenplay fast.' And he said to me, 'You've got to write it so that we can find out whether Willy is really serious about making this picture!'"

Finished in September 1963, Lehman delivered the script to Wyler. "After he'd gotten it, he called me up right away. He said 'Ernie, I'm embarrassed. I've never read such a wonderful first draft. I can't think of a single suggestion to make! There's nothing I can improve!' After I'd hung up, I called Dick. I said, 'Dick, we are in trouble. Willy's not going to make this picture. There's no such thing as Willy not being able to make suggestions!'"

Whatever doubts Lehman had, they would be proven correct the following week. Richard Zanuck had promptly sent the script to Rome, to his father Darryl, whose reaction was enthusiastic (with, naturally, the customary list of suggestions for changes). Meanwhile, Wyler had come forth to offer a few notes of his own. But Lehman remained suspicious.

Quite rightly so. The following week he was invited to a weekend party at Wyler's house in Malibu. The director was entertaining Rex Harrison and his wife, Rachel Roberts, and it was Wyler's suggestion that Lehman might help talk Harrison into playing the part of Captain von Trapp.

Lehman agreed. That afternoon he noted that his host and another guest, Mike Frankovich, the head of Columbia Pictures, were in an intense conference in a far corner of the living room. "The only way I can describe that scene is that they were in a huddle," said Lehman. And while Lehman went swimming with Harrison, to talk about the actor's possibly playing Captain von Trapp, the Wyler–Frankovich conversation continued. Lehman finally left the beach and returned to the house. In the living room, there were piles of scripts. "Everybody in town had been submitting scripts to Willy; they were everywhere I looked, face up — I could see all the titles. And then I came upon one script lying face down, so that you couldn't read the title. I flipped it over. It read: *The Collector—a Columbia Picture*. I turned it back so it was where I'd found it."

In the movie business, everyone specializes in knowing everything everyone else is doing. Lehman knew from reading the daily "trades" that *The Collector* was in preproduction at Columbia. Later it would be made in England, starring Terence Stamp and Samantha Eggar. Like a well-trained operative, Lehman put the facts together and came up with the solution. "When I got back home, I called Zanuck, and I said, 'Dick, Willy is going to direct *The Collector*. Be ready.'"

When Wyler's agent called the following week, Zanuck was ready. The agent, Paul Kohner, requested that Wyler be given the right to do *The Collector* before he went to work on *The Sound of Music*. Would Zanuck kindly postpone the Fox project until *The Collector* was finished? No, Zanuck would not. "You can tell your client we are not going to postpone our picture thirty seconds!" he told Kohner. "Let him go make *The Collector!*"

Which Wyler proceeded to do.

Why had they waited so long for Wyler to jump ship? "I guess it was very perverse of me," said Lehman. "I was willing to endure what I had to endure in order to get one of the best directors in the world. It's kind of like figuring out who your executioner would be. As it turned out, I guess I was pretty stupid, because, looking back on it, Willy wouldn't have been the best director for the picture."

"I think Willy got scared," was Richard Zanuck's opinion. "We all ranted and raved about how awful it was, what he'd pulled on us, but deep down inside, I was a bit relieved."

After the dust had settled and the shouting had died down, one immutable truth remained. It was October of 1963, and this project, which the Fox management was counting on being a success, had been in preproduction for ten months. If it were ever to be filmed, a new director was imperative.

Luckily, there was one who would be available.

The Sand Pebbles, the film project on which Robert Wise had been doing preproduction, had been delayed by the onset of the monsoon season in the Far East. Wise was sitting out the logistical problems those storms presented to his proposed shooting schedule. Learning of the director's problems, Lehman devised a quick end-run of his own. He called Wise's agent, Phil Gersh, and suggested sending a copy of the newly completed screenplay for Wise to read. Gersh demurred; hadn't Bob already indicated he wasn't interested? Wasn't Wyler supposed to be directing the picture?

"I told him: 'Phil, please, don't ask any questions, just give Bob my script,'" remembered Lehman. Gersh agreed, and the script went to Wise.

"Then my phone rang," said Lehman. "It was Dick Zanuck, who said, 'Come on down.' I went to his office. He said, 'I've got a surprise for you. What would you say if I told you we could get Bob Wise to direct this picture?'

"I said, 'Great!' He looked at me and smiled and said, 'You son of a bitch, you slipped him the script, didn't you?' And I said, 'Me? *Never!*'"

In fact, Wise had hesitated before making a commitment. He was sufficiently impressed with the screenplay to call on Saul Chaplin, his associate producer on *West Side Story* and an authority on filmed musical comedy. Would Chaplin enjoy working on this project? He needed his opinion.

"Saul," said Wise, "If you say yes, I'll say yes."

Both men shortly agreed on that monumental yes, but Chaplin also had his doubts initially. "It was a heavy responsibility," he remembered, years later. "I had seen the show in New York and hadn't liked it. It had that first-rate Rodgers and Hammerstein score, but the story was a bit too sweet for me. Then I read it. Before I began reading, I composed polite ways of expressing my objections. 'It's a helluva job, Ernie, but it's still too saccharine,' or 'Bob, it's an improvement over the play, but it's still not for you.'

"Then I read it. I was never so happy reading a script in my life. It was wonderful. Ernie had retained the elements that made the show such an enormous hit, but by changes and additions, he had improved it enormously. The characters were more clearly defined, it was more charming, and he had invented a truly exciting and suspenseful finish. Also, it read as if it had been written originally for the screen, instead of being an adaptation of a stage play," he recalled.

With both Wise and Chaplin agreeing to work on the project, after Lehman's intensive ten months' work on the script, it seemed finally as if the film version of *The Sound of Music* could be headed for the screen. A very wide screen, too; the Panavision filming in that magnificent Austrian landscape would in time bail out the shaky Twentieth Century-Fox empire.

Still, in 1964, such a happy ending was very much touch and go. In the cynical talk at the Beverly Hills dinner parties, and the gin rummy tables at Hillcrest, and on the greens at Bel-Air and Lakeside, people were down on the musical about a nun and a bunch of singing kids, all of them fleeing the Nazis across the Alps. Who needed that?

Who among those oh-so-shrewd naysayers could have imagined that Wise, Chaplin, Lehman, and Zanuck were about to create a classic? One that could be shown all over the world for decades to come, while throwing off an endless waterfall of golden profits far beyond any accountant's wildest imagination?

Three decades later, the same Saul Chaplin would sit in his Beverly Hills living room and remark, "Whenever those profit checks arrive, year after year, I look at the numbers and believe me, I'm always amazed!"

CHAPTER **8**

Verdant and Over Budget

The casting began. A difficult process, because there would be a large cast of characters to fill.

Beginning, of course, with Maria. Which actress would be the new sparkling, charming lead? Not Mary Martin. Years before, she'd decided she wasn't interested in re-creating her stage triumph. She'd brought the show to life, she'd played Maria for two years, and now she was on to other projects. And she and Dick Halliday had earned so much in profits from their ownership of *The Sound of Music* that she had taken the advice of her lawyer and her accountant — let them remain anonymous — to stop paying tax to the IRS and to sell her ownership for a final capital gain.

When one considers how much profit she'd have accrued over the years from her share of ownership in the film version, plus earnings from soundtrack albums, and so on, the mind boggles.

It would be Jack Warner, who'd dispatched Swifty Lazar to try to purchase the rights to *The Sound of Music*, in a back-door effort to keep the project dormant while his production of *My Fair Lady* went into the theatres, who proved to be, inadvertently perhaps, the matchmaker to provide Wise, Lehman, Zanuck et al. with their perfect leading lady.

In a monumentally wrong call, Warner had decided to find himself a major star for *My Fair Lady*. No matter that Julie Andrews had captivated New York audiences as the Eliza Doolittle of the original Lerner and Loewe production. Sure, she was talented, but she wasn't a big enough film star, Warner figured. So he passed on her as the lead, and to play opposite her Broadway leading man, Rex Harrison, he hired Audrey Hepburn instead. No matter that Hepburn wasn't a good singer, and that she'd have to be dubbed by Marni Nixon. Warner had his star insurance. Which left Julie Andrews in limbo.

Until Walt Disney decided she'd be the perfect lead opposite Dick Van Dyke in a musical version of *Mary Poppins.*

"We'd been tipped off how great she was in *Poppins,*" remembered Lehman. "So Bob and Saul and I went over to Disney and saw some footage from their picture. The minute we saw her, we all knew she was perfect for Maria von Trapp. 'Let's get her before somebody else does!' said Bob."

But Andrews wasn't sure she wanted to do the part. She was now in the midst of playing the lead in *The Americanization of Emily,* the film Wyler had thought of directing but eventually turned down. She was enjoying a nonmusical role; perhaps she'd continue doing such parts.

But the negotiations continued.

"Everyone from Audrey Hepburn to Anne Bancroft was mentioned for the part," said Chaplin. "The leading contender to play Captain von Trapp was Bing Crosby. He was the studio's suggestion, which we never really took seriously because we never considered him right for the part.

"Then there were the seven children," he remembered. "A conservative guess would be that about two hundred children were interviewed for those seven parts."

Before the casting was completed, Wise, Chaplin, and a production crew flew to Salzburg to scout locations. Following the notes that had been amassed by Lehman and Wyler on their previous trip, they looked at sites. In Lehman's descriptions for Maria's opening scenes among the Alps, he'd noted the site as *verdant.* So a running gag among Wise's crew was "Let's go find Ernie's *verdant.*"

But the mountains they wished to scout were covered in snow. Where up there should Maria, whoever she might be played by, sing her opening song? The local guide, hired as a production man, led the Americans to a large field knee-deep in snow and surrounded by tall trees, also cloaked in white. An opening song, to be shot high up in this frozen locale? Absolutely! "He assured us that at the time we planned to shoot, the field would be a lovely green," said Chaplin. "The verdant one Ernie had described for us in his script. I couldn't imagine how that was possible, but it turned out to be true."

While the crew was roaming the streets of old Salzburg, scouting other locations such as the venerable Nonnberg Abbey, where Maria Rainer was a postulant, there came news from far-off Hollywood. No less an authority than the all-powerful gossip columnist Louella Parsons had provided her readers with a scoop: Julie Andrews had been signed by Fox to play Maria!

"We were overjoyed and furious," remembered Chaplin. "Why did we have to find out about it in Parsons' column? It was a case of everyone at the studio assuming that someone else was going to let us know. In the meantime, we had wasted hours discussing other actresses who could play the part."

Now came the problem of casting Captain Georg von Trapp. Eventually, the choice would be the Broadway leading man Christopher Plummer. A fine classical actor, Plummer had hesitated at first. The role did not appeal to him; it provided him with no challenge. Years later, he said, "I wanted to give the Captain a little edge, a little humor. His character didn't have much substance. He came off as a fearful square. I wanted him to be equal to Maria."

He finally agreed to take on the role, but not before he'd been assured he and Lehman could meet to discuss the character he would portray. Then Plummer discovered his singing would be dubbed by another voice. He promptly decided such a process was demeaning. Let somebody else play Captain von Trapp!

"He said it robbed him of his masculinity," said Lehman. "I was on vacation, but I got a frantic call to come back immediately; I had to try to get Plummer back for the project. After a lot of phone calls, Chris agreed to come over to my office, and we sat down for a few days, and we began to go over his scenes, one by one."

Lehman had made himself a note regarding von Trapp's screen character. "Captain and Elsa," it said. "More familiar with each other — they joke with each other — charming, intimate, and evasive — light, witty and amusing. Captain is comfortable with Elsa."

With that as a starting point, Lehman and Plummer would work together for the ensuing week, making changes in the Captain's character. "I've never worked with an actor who is so intelligent about how his scenes would work," Lehman commented later. "This guy was insisting that I be a good writer. So he came off better than before. And he *helped* me!"

William Luce, the author of Plummer's enormously successful one-man show of the late 1990s, *Barrymore* (in which he played the great actor John Barrymore), echoed Lehman's experience. "Plummer is a classically trained pianist," Luce observed. "I've seen how he intuitively feels in the dialogue the dynamics of music. While working on *Barrymore*, he would say, 'There's one syllable too many in this line.' Only a poet or a musician would say that."

So with the revisions he and Lehman had agreed upon in the script, Plummer was willing to play Captain von Trapp. But there was still the problem of his singing. Why should he agree to have his voice dubbed? It was finally agreed that Plummer would be permitted to sing his own songs. "We agreed with his agent to have him do so," said Lehman. "Then we figured we'd show him the rushes of himself, to prove that his voice wasn't absolutely right. And when we'd finished with this process, guess what? Plummer's voice was finally replaced by a dubbing, the way we'd wanted to do it in the first place."

Before the film was considered ready for production, however, there were changes made in Rodgers and Hammerstein's score. "My Favorite Things," which had been sung onstage by the Abbess to Maria, would now be filmed as a sequence between Maria and the children. And "The Lonely Goatherd" would be used as the basis for a delightful puppet-show sequence.

Then came the problem of two songs in the score that Rodgers and Hammerstein had written for Max and Elsa, "How Can Love Survive?" and "No Way to Stop It." In Lehman's adaptation, Max had a far more aggressive role, and Elsa certainly as much, if not more so, in her near-romance with the Captain. Thus, their somewhat cynical attitudes toward life, and the joys of being surrounded by the upper class, and the advantages of the status quo, as expressed in Hammerstein's original lyrics, did not jibe well with their altered characters.

And the duet between the Captain and Maria, "An Ordinary Couple," so gentle and quiet, now seemed far too muted for their romantic involvement. Certainly the two characters played by Julie Andrews and Christopher Plummer were far from being ordinary!

Chaplin and Wise flew to New York to consult with Rodgers on the changes they contemplated for the film. Might he consider writing a ballad for the two leads, to replace "An Ordinary Couple"? Rodgers was in total agreement. The song should obviously be replaced; in fact, he and Hammerstein had discussed such a change, but the lyricist, alas, had been too ill to do the work.

The second suggestion offered by Wise and Chaplin was for Maria, a solo number beginning when she departed from the abbey to go to the Captain's mansion. Might it be a soliloquy in which Maria expresses her feelings as she travels toward her new life?

"I described what I hoped the song might be about," said Chaplin. "She leaves the abbey and is fearful of facing the outside world alone, yet it is God's will — she must obey. She believes everything in life has a purpose, so perhaps her fears are groundless. Gradually, as she moves on through her journey, she convinces herself that it will all turn out fine. By the time she reaches the villa, she is looking forward to this new challenge."

Rodgers went to his piano and commenced writing both the melody and the lyrics for two new numbers. Soon he had completed a new song for Maria and the Captain, "Something Good." Both Wise and Chaplin received it with enthusiasm; it was obviously right for the film.

Rodgers had also written a soliloquy for Maria; its title was "I Have Confidence." This wasn't exactly what Chaplin had suggested; it seemed too brief. There ensued a series of communications back and forth. Rodgers rewrote his original number; but once again, it didn't seem quite sufficient. Chaplin felt it needed an inner progression, one in which the audience could see how Maria would go from being unsure to growing in self-reliance, and finally displaying high-spirited optimism.

After several more tries, Rodgers completed his version. Once again, it wasn't quite what Wise and Chaplin had contemplated.

Rodgers finally suggested to Chaplin, since he was so clear on what was needed, that he try to rewrite the song himself. Reluctantly, Chaplin agreed to put together a version based completely on Rodgers's music, in an arrangement to make the proper progression. "I was determined not to write it myself," said Chaplin, "because I am no Richard Rodgers!"

Chaplin promptly went to work with Lehman to put together lyrics and set them to Rodgers's melody for "I Have Confidence." Chaplin cleverly included the verse to "The Sound of Music" that wasn't yet being used in the film. The second section of the soliloquy was pure Rodgers, and then it was followed by a third section, a reprise of Rodgers' music with additional lyrics. That would be the final version of "I Have Confidence."

Throughout this delicate process, Julie Andrews would continue to question Chaplin: What was happening with her new soliloquy?

"I invented all sorts of excuses," confessed Chaplin. "I didn't want her to know we were asking her to sing a song which was not as written by Rodgers. And, in any case, before she heard it I had to get Rodgers' permission to use it in the picture." He brought in Marni Nixon, swore her to secrecy, and had her record the number. The recording went off to the composer in New York. A day later there came Rodgers's telegram reply. He preferred his version of "I Have Confidence," but since the revised version seemed to be the choice of the filmmakers, he would give it his official okay.

The soliloquy went into the film. "Postscript," added Chaplin, "Julie didn't know how her number had come about until about two years later, after the picture was released, when I felt it was safe to tell her."

Years later, he remembered, "Working with Julie Andrews reminded me of working with Judy Garland. They both learned music instantly, as if by magic. They both made songs sound better than you imagined they could. Both made suggestions about how a song should be sung, and if their ideas were rejected, they accepted the rejection gracefully. They had great objectivity about their own work, and knew when they had done well. And they were very bright and fun to be with."

The Sound of Music began shooting in Hollywood, at the Fox studio, on March 23, 1964 — at last.

The first sequences were interiors, done on the Fox sound stages. "Marc Breaux and I left for Salzburg a week before the rest of the company," said

Chaplin. Breaux and his wife, Dee Dee, had been assigned to choreograph the film. "We'd pre-recorded two numbers, 'Do-Re-Mi' and 'I Have Confidence,' which we'd planned to shoot on the streets and environs of Salzburg. We put both tracks on a portable tape recorder, and took them out to test the numbers on the actual locations, to see whether or not we had gotten them right for time. If the length of the music had to be changed, then the studio could adjust the music tracks before the rest of the company left for Salzburg."

That Chaplin and Breaux were not killed was a miracle. The first time they went out to test their timings, they hadn't counted on the traffic flow during daytime hours. "We would both stand at the top of the street where the action was to start and wait for the traffic light to turn red. The moment it did, I turned on the tape, loud, and Marc would go down the street, dancing. Unfortunately, the traffic lights had no regard for the length of our playbacks. Often, they'd go green before our music had run out. Then it became a matter of dodging the traffic to stay alive! The onlookers thought we were crazy."

Finally, the cast and crew arrived in Salzburg and went to work to film the von Trapp story, right where it had happened. That production manager who'd previously helped scout locations had known what he was about, and that snowy site he'd chosen for Julie Andrews's opening scene was high, impressive, and quite verdant. Breathtakingly so.

But when it came to weather, no production manager could have foreseen what would ensue. It was to be a very wet summer. "It isn't just that it rained," said Chaplin. "It often rained aggravatingly. We could come down to breakfast at 7 a.m., the weather sparkling, nothing but blue skies up above. ... We would get into our cars and head for our location, happily jabbering away. By the time we reached our destination, we would be in the middle of a torrential downpour! We would sit around on location all day, waiting for the sun to reappear. A few times, it did, too late to start shooting. But the sunny days compensated for the waiting."

Later, there would be an ironic aspect to that wet summer Wise and his crew struggled through. When the film was out and playing in theatres, Fox would receive all sorts of mail from moviegoers who were confused by their experience. They'd loved seeing *The Sound of Music*; they'd been enormously impressed by the beauty of medieval Salzburg, and they'd gone to visit that city while on holiday. But somehow they must have picked the wrong time to go "because it rained quite a bit while we were there!"

These and other unforeseen delays meant that when the cast and crew finally returned to Hollywood, the film was well over its original budget. One of the Fox executives confronted Chaplin with this problem. Did he realize how much more the film was costing? Of course Chaplin did; for an associate producer, such matters were a daily headache.

"But have you seen how beautiful the film is?" he asked.

"Yes, but what's important now is: Do you think you could talk to Wise about shooting faster, so we can make up for some lost time?" asked the studio executive.

"Without even blinking, I replied, 'I'll try,'" said Chaplin.

"Although I said it, I hadn't the slightest intention of even mentioning the conversation to Bob, and I never have. He knew better than I how far behind we were. My talking to him about it would have accomplished nothing. Bob's films were always so masterfully created," added Chaplin, "that we stayed out of his way. The film finally did finish, considerably over budget, but history has since proved it to be a sound investment indeed."

Which may be one of the great understatements of our time.

Postproduction work began in the fall. There were weeks of dubbing, looping, and editing, all meticulously carried out under Wise's supervision. He'd begun his career years back at RKO, working for the legendary Val Lewton as an editor. In the film world, he was considered a master of his craft.

Meanwhile, Irwin Kostal, who'd been hired as music director, went to work to do the film score.

Finally, in February, there would be a "sneak" preview.

Wise had always been an advocate for such an event. For the finishing touches to the film, he felt audience input was vital. He'd written Zanuck a memo extolling the value of such a process. "We spend years, much effort, and millions of dollars getting a picture on film, and then, so often, we don't spend the additional time and effort to give it the proper acid test before a nonprofessional audience."

That first preview would take place in middle America, far away in Minneapolis, in circumstances that would be less an acid test than an endurance contest.

At the Mann Theatre, on February 1, 1965, there was typical Minnesota weather. It was about thirty degrees below zero. But outside, an audience was patiently standing in line, waiting to be permitted into the theatre.

Their reaction was universally enthusiastic. According to Zanuck, the response was incredible: "They even gave us a standing ovation at the intermission!"

When the audience reaction cards had been inspected, the comments were a steady stream of *Excellent*. There were three cards that merely indicated *Good*. "Suddenly, we were focusing on those three cards, trying to figure out what we did wrong!" commented Zanuck.

The second preview, in Tulsa, Oklahoma, was very different. The theatre managers opened the box office late; the Oklahomans had been standing in line in freezing weather. When the people finally got inside the theatre, they were in an aggressive mood.

Thus, the opening sequence of the film, as the camera moves in silence across the impressive Alpine landscape, met with an angry reaction. "The audience assumed there was something wrong with the sound system, I guess," remembered Chaplin. "They started cat-calling, then they booed and yelled, all through the opening. It was pandemonium ... and finally, they quieted down when, on the screen, Julie had begun her number."

When the film ended, there were cheers and applause.

But the future was still iffy.

Would *The Sound of Music* be the big hit picture which Twentieth Century-Fox so desperately needed? "I remember, when that preview was over," said Chaplin, "Mike Kaplan was talking about the reaction, and he said, 'Make no mistake about it: This is much more than a musical hit. This is going to be a *classic*.'" He correctly echoed Hammerstein's prediction about the stage version six years earlier.

But then, it was his job as a press agent for Fox to be an optimist, right? So who could believe *him*?

Figure 8.1 Richard Rodgers and Julie Andrews smile for the photographers at the premiere showing of *The Sound of Music* in New York. (Courtesy of Photofest)

CHAPTER **9**
Triumph Again

The film of *The Sound of Music,* on which the future existence of Twentieth Century-Fox films depended, opened in Manhattan at the Rivoli Theatre, on March 2, 1965.

While the invited premiere audience of New Yorkers sat through the first unreeling of the film on which so much time and effort had been lavished, Robert Wise sneaked out of the theatre and went to the lobby, where he met with Jonas Rosenfeld, Fox's head of publicity.

Rosenfeld had obtained an advance copy of Bosley Crowther's *New York Times* review of the following morning. Crowther was a major power in film criticism; from his office typewriter on West 43rd Street came daily the most important verdicts on films, domestic and foreign.

Inside, the Rivoli opening-night audience could be heard through the lobby doors as they applauded and enjoyed the film. Standing in the lobby, the two men read:

> The great big color movie Mr. Wise has made from the play ... comes close to being a careful duplication of the show as it was done on the stage, even down to its operetta pattern, which predates the cinema age. ... Julie Andrews provides the most apparent and fetching innovation in the film. ... Her role is always in peril of collapsing under the weight of romantic nonsense and sentiment.

Then came the true bashing.

> The septet of blonde and beaming youngsters who have to act like so many Shirley Temples and Freddy Bartholomews when they were young, do as well as could be expected with their assortedly artificial

roles ... but the adults are fairly horrendous, especially Christopher Plummer. ... The movie is staged by Mr. Wise in a cosy-cum-corny fashion that even theatre people know is old hat. ... *The Sound of Music* repeats, in style — and in theme.

And so on. The stunned Wise and Rosenfeld must have wondered if they were in the right theatre.

The following morning, Judith Crist of the *Herald-Tribune* took careful aim at *The Sound of Music* and fired. The title of her review was an eye-catcher: "If You Have Diabetes, Stay Away from This Movie."

On went the bashing. "Everything is so icky-sticky purely ever-lovin' that even Constant Andrews Admirers will get a wittle woozy long before intermission time," Crist moaned. "There is nothing like a super-sized screen to convert seven darling little kids in no time at all into all that W. C. Fields indicated that darling little kids are — which is pure loathsome. The movie is for the five to seven set, and their mommies, who think their kids aren't up to the stinging sophistication and biting wit of *Mary Poppins*."

If that weren't sufficient, Crist, who was also the resident film critic on the NBC *Today* show, would repeat her opinion to a far vaster national audience.

That would induce the restored grand panjandrum of Fox, Darryl Zanuck, to send an angry memo to one of his executives, in which he blazed back at Crist with both guns. "She has built her reputation with a knife and the evil skill of an abortionist!" he declared. "She uses the tactics of a concentration camp butcher!"

However, when his underling responded by suggesting enthusiastically that they spearhead an attempt to remove Crist from her NBC position, Zanuck controlled his rage. "While I would thoroughly enjoy the pleasure of inserting the toe of my ski boot in Miss Crist's derriere," he replied, "I prefer to leave the job to moviegoers, who, in due time, will take good care of her."

For once, Zanuck had controlled his temper; his decision to do so would prove remarkably tactful. Crist remembered years later, "My review was also reprinted in the *Paris Herald,* and when it appeared, I got hate mail from all over the world!"

The shock of those bad reviews was tough to handle. Lehman and Wise commiserated, while the New York critics continued their barrage. In the *New Yorker,* Brendan Gill wrote, "A huge, tasteless blow-up of the celebrated musical. Even the handful of authentic location shots have a hokey studio sheen. I felt myself slowly drowning in a pit of sticky-sweet whipped cream, not of the first freshness."

And in *McCall's,* Pauline Kael also fired a salvo. "*The Sound of Music* is the sugar-coated lie that people seem to want to eat ... and this is the attitude that makes a critic feel that maybe it's all hopeless. ... Why not just send the director, Robert Wise, a wire: 'You win. I give up.'"

As they had with Judith Crist, the ever-growing phalanx of faithful fans would retaliate: they deluged the *McCall's* editorial office with angry letters protesting Kael's scorn. So vehement was the *McCall's* readers' rebellion that it impelled the editors to take action. Since Kael seemed so obviously out of touch with their readers' tastes, they went looking for her replacement, someone less acerbically disturbing to their paying customers, and she was let go (a remarkable statement about the position of criticism in that magazine's pages).

Pauline Kael went on to the *New Yorker,* while *The Sound of Music* went on to its California openings. There, remarkably, the film met with almost universal approval. Years later, Wise would comment, "The East Coast intellectual papers and magazines destroyed us, but the local papers and the trades out here gave us great reviews."

Many years back, a shrewd writer named Hopkins, who was employed at MGM, ad-libbed a phrase: he said of a certain producer known for his lack of talent that "his criticisms had all the impact of a mouse peeing on a blotter." So it was with the criticisms of *The Sound of Music.*

Consider what had happened in London, after the stage show opened in 1961. Hadn't those acerbic critics taken aim and vented their spleen upon the show? Remember Bernard Levin's assessment: "A marsh of treacle, bathed in a dim religious light"? Or Harold Hobson, insisting "It is a mistake to treat the von Trapps as heroes"? And what of W. A. Darlington, with his line about "Austrian sugar icing an inch thick"? Those tirades had been printed, and now, four years later, satisfied British theatregoers were packing the seats at the Palace Theatre for eight performances a week. By now, the show was on its way to becoming the longest-running musical ever to play London.

And it would continue to pack in the audience even *after* the Fox movie version of *The Sound of Music* opened as a two-a-day attraction, three short blocks away — even though common theatrical knowledge dictated that the presence of Julie Andrews in the film would destroy the audience's appetite for live performances of the show. Not bloody likely! London would be treated to the remarkable phenomenon of the play *and* the film version of the play, running in tandem, week after week, to full houses.

One loyal *Sound of Music* fan, Mrs. Myra Franklin, came religiously to see the film at a Monday matinee, once a week, in the same seat, for the entire run of the film! Obviously she agreed with that shrewd fellow Hopkins at MGM with respect to Bernard Levin's critique.

Bashing *The Sound of Music* was not only the fashionable territory of scornful critics and sophisticated naysayers, but of professional cynics in all quarters. Was it not Christopher Plummer himself who was famous in show business for his suggestion that the film in which he had starred be retitled *The Sound of Mucus*? And in that same interview, did he not suggest that "practically anyone could write a musical about nuns and children, and have it become a success"?

"How interesting," replied Russel Crouse, when he was apprised of Plummer's observation. "I wonder why nobody ever did it?"

From California, in 1965, it was *Daily Variety's* savvy critic who delivered the most cogent assessment of the film: it "bears the mark of assured lengthy runs ... and should be one of the season's most successful entries."

The Sound of Music quickly went out to play in 131 American theatres as a "road-show" attraction. The road-show was a time-honored Hollywood marketing ploy that dates back to the early silent days. Films with the size and status of *Birth of a Nation, Ben-Hur,* and *King of Kings* were played in large theatres on a two-a-day schedule, with impressive hoopla, and tickets were sold on a reserved-seat basis.

In the summer of 1965, Twentieth Century-Fox needed an infusion of capital desperately and took a gamble. The company also had its other two blockbusters — *The Agony and the Ecstasy,* from Italy, and *Those Magnificent Men in Their Flying Machines,* from England — as possible road-show attractions to play in large theatres where the projection system could accommodate a 70mm-wide print accompanied by a stereophonic soundtrack. The studio sent all three attractions out to the public. The gamble paid off better than the wildest Las Vegas winning streak.

Audiences loved them — especially *The Sound of Music* — and paid no attention to its bad reviews. They loved the Rodgers and Hammerstein score, and the Lindsay and Crouse libretto that Lehman had so lovingly adapted and Wise had so skillfully directed. They loved Julie Andrews, they loved the Alps, they loved the children. Within four short road-show weeks, the film became number one in gross receipts at the American box office. For the next four and a half years it would retain that position, and then become *Variety's* all-time box office champion in rentals derived from the U.S. and Canadian market.

And, in the words of another classic Hammerstein character, Cap'n Andy of *Show Boat*: "That's only the beginning, folks, only the beginning!"

Years later Saul Chaplin said, "None of us anticipated what a wildfire hit the film would be, particularly after it received such mixed reviews from the critics. Now it just throws off those remarkable profit checks." Beamed Chaplin: "Go figure."

At Academy Award time, *The Sound of Music* was nominated in ten categories. The film was nominated for Best Picture, Robert Wise for Best Director, and Julie Andrews for Best Actress.

The results of the voting would be, putting it mildly, confusing. After the fanfare, the oohs and ahs at the spectacular gowns, the introductions, and the oh-gosh-I-want-to-thank-all-those-who-helped-me-make-this-happen acceptance speeches, *The Sound of Music* won for Best Editing, Best Sound, and Best Scoring of a Musical.

Irwin Kostal won the last. Saul Chaplin reported that Kostal approached him, Oscar in hand, and said, "We should be sharing this! I don't know why you didn't hand your name in with mine!" Chaplin demurred; for years he'd decided if he received any producer credit, he'd forgo that music credit, "even though my contribution might have merited it," he added modestly.

Julie Andrews had already won a Best Actress Oscar previously, for *Mary Poppins,* and on this occasion she lost to Julie Christie, who'd played the lead in *Darling.* When the Best Director award came up, the winner was Robert Wise. Andrews came up from the audience to accept on Wise's behalf. The director was in Taiwan, wrestling with the formidable difficulties involved in completing *The Sand Pebbles.* As Andrews stood on the stage, she received an enormous accolade from the audience. Was there, perhaps, some disagreement over her loss this year?

Then, finally, came the Best Picture award ...

The Sound of Music!

Who can make sense of the ins and outs of Academy Award voters? And how to explain the conspicuous absence from the Best Screenplay award of Ernie Lehman's carefully crafted adaptation?

In effect, the voters were saying that the winning edifice had been built without a blueprint. Wise, who certainly knew better, wrote to Lehman from Taiwan. (Lehman, by that time, was wrestling with his own formidable difficulties, making the Warner Brothers film of Edward Albee's *Who's Afraid of Virginia Woolf?* starring Elizabeth Taylor and Richard Burton.) "All I can say," wrote Wise, "is *you was robbed.* I guess that's one of the prices that the writer — and some of the others connected with making the picture — pays for taking an established Broadway show and transposing it to the screen."

Lehman responded, "I value your letter very much. The enormous success of the picture all over the world and my own realization ... that I guessed right in believing that the play would become a very rewarding and popular film ... that I actually did have an important role in getting it from stage to screen ... make it very difficult for me to have any unhappy feelings about anything connected with this picture. ... When you stop to consider what we achieved ... this miracle that comes only to a very few, once in a lifetime ... well, out with the champagne!"

Thirty-odd years later, Lehman reflected on the writer's lot: "Funny, every few weeks, I get called by some TV producer or documentary outfit ... and they're putting together some retrospective, on Bob Wise, or Burt Lancaster, or any of the stars or directors I've worked with. And they want some sort of a firsthand comment from me. But you know something? They never seem to do a documentary about a writer." He smiled. "At least, not one I've heard about."

The film's worldwide success — by the time this history is being written, the gross has mounted to, according to *Variety*, $293,600,000 worldwide — is even more spectacular when one considers that at the time of its production, American film musicals had fallen upon hard times in European and Asian markets. Why? Consider the problem of dubbing American films. An ordinary thriller, a spectacle, or a love story presents no problems when it comes to reaching international audiences. Go into a studio with actors, dub a film into foreign languages, or add subtitles, and presto! the audience in South America, the Far East, or Middle Europe can enjoy it. But when it comes to musicals, the problems are tremendous.

"The songs in most musicals were left in English, and there would be subtitles added at the bottom of the screen," explained Saul Chaplin. "But having to read those subtitles during the songs annoyed foreign audiences, and detracted from their enjoyment of the film. Can you blame them for preferring Sly Stallone?"

Since *The Sound of Music* was such a big draw domestically, Fox executives shrewdly decided that both the songs and the dialogue should be dubbed into various languages. Chaplin was sent to Paris, Barcelona, Rome, and Berlin with the assignment to supervise the dubbing of the songs and to reproduce the energy and the spirit of the original soundtrack, which turned out to be a very complex task.

First, there needed to be translations of the Hammerstein lyrics. Sounds simple. Perhaps, until you come to a song like "Do-Re-Mi," for one example. The scale, as Chaplin pointed out — do, re, mi — exists in all languages, so it can be retained. But then the Hammerstein lyrics begin with "Doe, a deer, a female deer." "While 'doe' means female deer in English," sighed Chaplin, "it doesn't in any other language. So, not only did a substitute have to be found in each of the four other languages for every note of the scale, but the translations had to be in sync with what Julie and the children were singing."

Perhaps the meticulous work done in translating Hammerstein's lyrics helped make the film version of *The Sound of Music* the remarkable and lasting triumph that it was all over the world. Years after its production, Ernest Lehman expressed some wonder at this overwhelming success, which crosses borders and languages everywhere. He shrugged: "Who sits down and says, 'Now we're going to make a classic'?" Then, recalling how he first reacted to the Mary Martin production on Broadway and, over that intermission bowl of Howard Johnson's chowder, believed it might make a successful film, he said: "When I see the picture today, I have a lot of respect for it. People love this picture. ... Bob Wise shot it beautifully. Every frame works! And the story has universality. I think in some way it taps into every audience's emotional response."

Everywhere, that is, except for two countries: Germany and Austria, where the movie's returns are not as hefty. "The Austrians never understood why we were making another film about the von Trapps, since the Germans had already done so," said Chaplin. "But the primary reason was that the last third of our picture dealt with their Nazi past. Neither the Austrians nor the Germans liked to be reminded of that period. In fact, Fox's German manager took it upon himself to delete the last third of the film, which completely eliminated all the Nazis!"

What could be the result of that minor putsch?

"The Fox studio people in L.A. learned about that very quickly," grinned Chaplin. "Fired the manager, and had the film restored to its original length."

One postscript to this saga: the enormous success of *The Sound of Music* prompted other studios to follow the age-old Hollywood tradition — always try copying a hit. Large, expensive musicals once again became the order of the day. Out of the studios came *Fiddler on the Roof, Man of La Mancha, Doctor Dolittle,* and so on. Millions of dollars went into their production, and into the theatres they came, singing and dancing. And what became of all those expensive blockbuster musicals?

They all died.

Robert Wise's next musical venture would be one of those very expensive wide-screen productions. It seemed like a natural: Julie Andrews portraying the legendary British musical comedy performer Gertrude Lawrence. Lavish production numbers set to wonderful music by Noël Coward, Cole Porter, Kurt Weill, with their sparkling lyrics. Enthusiastically underwritten by Twentieth Century-Fox — with Saul Chaplin as Wise's ever-reliable coproducer.

Did lightning strike twice?

Hardly. You just might see that dazzling movie, *Star!,* every once in a while on television, or rent it from your videotape library, if they carry it at all.

Meanwhile, Rodgers and Hammerstein's finale continues to be a grand one.

This brings us full circle. The show-business magic cannot be lost on us: just as the great team's first risk-taking show, *Oklahoma!,* had brought the Theatre Guild back from the brink of financial disaster, their final, unrevolutionary one saved a major Hollywood studio from ruin. The movie continues to play to large and adoring audiences everywhere, year after year — but then ...

So does the Broadway show.

CHAPTER **10**
Revival

It's forty years and counting now since the night at the New Haven Shubert when the curtain rose for the first time to reveal those nuns at the Nonnberg Abbey, as they sang their beautiful opening "Preludium." Forty theatrical seasons of steady weekly grosses, pouring in from packed houses of ticket holders, here and abroad, who've sat enthralled through the drama of the von Trapps and come up the aisles humming "Edelweiss," or chanting "Doe, a deer ... ," who've brought home the sheet music or the LP, or the CD, to play over and over, whose children have danced around the room singing "My Favorite Things." Generations who know Maria's story from having seen the movie — not once, but often — who've snatched up the videotape as soon as it surfaced at the mall, and who've brought it home to sit before the TV, with their family, absorbed by the romance of the nun and the naval captain, and whose offspring have empathized with those brave von Trapp children, as they wave and sing, "So Long, Farewell."

While paying not the slightest attention to anyone who might suggest that they've already seen this videotape so many times that they know it all by heart!

For what does it matter how often you've seen *The Sound of Music*? If you loved it the first time, it's a lifetime romance, not only for you but for your kids, and probably their offspring as well.

A phenomenon, indeed, considering the bad notices the show met with! As we shall see, the show continues to be denigrated critically. Balance that with Oscar Hammerstein, at the second performance, predicting: "Make no mistake about it, this is a hit!": the words of a master.

Summer stock? Touring companies? High school and college theatres? Been there, and continues to do that, that, and that. In fact, *The Sound of Music* and *Oklahoma!* are the two most popular musicals in the Rodgers and Hammerstein catalogue. Over the years since 1960, more than 17,500 stock and amateur productions of *The Sound of Music* have been licensed. So where do we go from here?

Back to Broadway, of course — in a major revival produced in 1998 by Hallmark Entertainment.

It had a new leading lady to play Maria, the ravishing Rebecca Luker, a tall blonde who was one of the leads in the 1997 revival of *Show Boat*, and it was directed by Susan H. Shulman, who also directed Luker on Broadway in the 1991 musical success *The Secret Garden*, and also in a revival of Rodgers and Hart's *The Boys from Syracuse* (in an "Encores" series of concert-style presentations at Manhattan's City Center).

Chatting about her remounting of Rodgers and Hammerstein's last show, Shulman was lavish in her praise of Luker's talent: "During her audition," she recalled, "Rebecca brought such a freshness to the music ... little hairs stood up on the back of my neck. You don't expect songs that you are so familiar with to take you by surprise that way."

Add Luker to the category of longtime *Sound of Music* fans. "My mother dragged me to the movie when I was nine years old," she proudly related, "and two years later, I sang 'My Favorite Things' in a talent show, and won first prize!"

Never underestimate the power of an advertising man's mind. Some brilliant agency thinker, perhaps picking up on his own offspring's zeal, has created TV spots for the revival in which we see a mother and daughter; the mother is reminiscing about having seen the show as a child, and the response from the daughter is "Do I get my own ticket?"

Don't bet she won't.

Of course, director Shulman is also an enthusiast. "As I've been telling people that I'm doing this show — people that you know must be part of the New York intelligentsia and who you might think would be snobbish about it and ask me, 'What are you doing that for?' — no, indeed, I get: 'Oh, I'm so excited, that's my favorite show! I'm in theatre because of it. It was my first musical!' Or they say: 'I saw the movie and that made me want to become involved in musical theatre!' People I never dreamt would have that response."

She noted that during one recent summer prior to the revival, a screening of *The Sound of Music* was run in Bryant Park, near Times Square, admission-free. Huge crowds turned out for it. "The response to the movie was as if they were at some rock concert!" said Shulman. "They were applauding, and yelling, and screaming for everything that happened up on the screen. And singing the score, as well!

"Somebody recently gave me an article about Caroline Kennedy's fortieth birthday," she added. "The whole gist of the story was that *The Sound of Music* is her favorite musical, and for her birthday, Julie Andrews herself came to the party and sang to her."

So how does Shulman approach the revisiting of this classic musical work, this icon?

She is well aware of the changes since 1959 in audience attitude concerning the underlying Trapp Family story. The Mary Martin production had occurred in the days when there was a subtle de-Nazification in the theatre. Listen to Theodore Bikel: "As the show came closer to Broadway from Boston, the Nazi uniforms got lighter and lighter. And by the time we arrived at the Lunt-Fontanne Theatre, there wasn't an armband or a swastika on anyone."

Certainly not, back then. In those days, with Mary Martin heading the cast, director Vincent Donehue and the creative minds he was working with were concentrating on the creation of a typical star-driven New York entertainment, not a polemic. Even though Hammerstein, Rodgers, Lindsay, and Crouse were all avowed anti-Nazis, they were all creating, first and foremost, a theatre piece.

But this time, in 1998, the show was being staged in an era when Swiss bank accounts were being cracked open to reveal gold and money hidden for half a century from desperate Jewish refugees, and when art treasures stolen by the Nazis all over Europe were being reclaimed from museums by the descendants of their rightful owners. After three decades of profound dramatizations of the Holocaust, audiences seem to be interested as much in truth as in entertainment. The 1955 stage play *The Diary of Anne Frank*, revised for a restaging during the same year, underscored the bestial cruelty of the Nazi regime. And yet another concurrent revival, the Kander and Ebb musical *Cabaret*, was being staged to inject a harsher-than-ever reality into its portrait of the decadence of 1930s Berlin.

This is the time, then, to reexamine *The Sound of Music*, is it not?

"Absolutely," affirmed Shulman. "If you do the show today, you must be historically accurate ... or else it becomes frivolous. And this is not a frivolous story. The courage of the von Trapps, in the light of the ugly events taking place in their beloved Salzburg, is truly profound.

"It must have been such a dreadful shock," she observed. "Right up until the Nazi takeover, the Anschluss, in Salzburg the mayor lied to the people. He told them the Nazis weren't coming. The next day, the Nazis moved in; the people watched their city being taken over ... and the mayor said he was sorry."

The day the Nazi forces took over, Nazi flags were draped everywhere — as they will be, she explained, on the set of the revival in the second act. "So when Captain von Trapp refuses to fly that flag, it's no small gesture. He was a wealthy man, a man of no small position. He could easily have collaborated with the Nazis, but no, he chose to leave, taking his family with him. ... It was an extremely courageous act.

"I'm in no way rewriting this show," Shulman pointed out. "You could say I've simply been digging into it."

To begin with, she and her scenic designer, Heidi Ettinger, traveled to Salzburg, taking with them a list (provided by Julie Andrews) of sights that were must-sees. "That scenery is so spectacular," she declared. "And when the weather is good, everyone immediately goes outdoors. The time we spent immersing ourselves in that remarkable city was most helpful to our eventual concept. Everywhere you look, if you're in Salzburg below, there are those magnificent Alps all around you. They can seem beautiful and inviting, and then they can also seem ominous and scary." As Maria says in the script, "I thought these mountains were my friends, and now they are my enemies." "That's the feeling I'm trying to impart," said Shulman. "That ominous feeling of a world sitting on a precipice, on something so potentially dangerous."

This inevitably brings us to the question of what the director believes is the reason that *The Sound of Music* has had such a lasting impact on its audiences, wherever it has played.

Said Shulman: "I think that's quite simple to explain. At its heart, it's a great love story. A May–December romance. If you believe that great musicals are always great love stories, as I do, that's got to be it. ... And this story comes with an amazingly good score that's very accessible. People of every age can remember those songs. It's an inspirational family show. And I mean that in the most positive sense."

Sixty years to the day after Hitler's forces marched into Salzburg, on the night of March 12, *The Sound of Music* opened at the Martin Beck Theatre on West 45th Street.

"It's a perfect theatre for the show," said Shulman. "Because the theatre itself looks exactly like Nonnberg Abbey. When we walked in there, I thought, 'How could any house be more perfect?' Once you're inside, it has a very Gothic character to it."

In March 1999, a star, Richard Chamberlain, joined the cast of this remounting — playing Captain von Trapp, of course — and it was announced that he would go on the production's national tour.

Quite a revival!

And a box-office hit, naturally. On the weekend following the Thursday-night opening of the revival, the box office at the Martin Beck sold more than half a million dollars' worth of tickets.

Shall we, then, pick up our theme once again, of the critics versus the audience? Here are the inevitable New York reviews, and some other comments, on *The Sound of Music*, circa 1998:

Ben Brantley, *The New York Times*

This latest version of Rodgers and Hammerstein's final collaboration is the first to be mounted on Broadway since 1959. But despite the refreshing presence of its star, Rebecca Luker, and a perfectly respectable production, it remains the same old cup of treacle. Whether performed in a church basement, or a show palace, *The Sound of Music* will always on some level, work; on another, it will always nauseate. ...

The director does underscore the threat of Nazism in the show ... but this mostly registers as just shorthand for indicating evil against the forces of light. ... This is not the imagery of politics, but of fairy tales. ...

But face it, *The Sound of Music* isn't really for grown-ups. ... Indeed, as a fable-like adventure story about reclaiming a lost father and gaining a fun-loving mother, it seems to strike deep responsive chords in the very young. ...

I can personally confirm this, having seen the movie at least half a dozen times when I was 10, and I know every lyric by heart. ... [I] can't say I rediscovered that inner child watching this version; frankly, it seemed endless. On the other hand, the little girl two seats down from me had a look of religious rapture on her face.

Clive Barnes, *The New York Post*

The Sound of Music is not for Do Re Me.

It's almost as bad as confessing you don't like peanut butter and jelly. ...

However, *The Sound of Music*, which last night was given a spic-and-span and spanking new production, is never going to be one of my favorite things ... any more than those damned "Bright copper kettles" they sing about.

I try to love it the way many people love it. But it doesn't help me. The mind is willing, but the heart is weak. ... So it's something of a necessary guess, but I imagine that if you love *The Sound of Music*, this is

The Sound of Music you will almost certainly love. If you don't love *The Sound of Music*, well, the issue is probably irrelevant, isn't it?

But when the *New York Post* asked after the preview performance, "Did you like *The Sound of Music*?" an audience member replied: "I liked it more than anything I've ever seen on Broadway!" (Diane Russo, East Brunswick, New Jersey).

Donald Lyons, *The Wall Street Journal*

The Sound of Music is splendid entertainment. Back for the first time since its initial run, the new production echoes less the play than the widely beloved 1965 movie, which starred Julie Andrews and opened up the story spectacularly. This is, under Susan H. Shulman's fresh and clear direction, a *Sound of Music* lit throughout by a warm and infectious generosity of spirit.

David Patrick Stearns, *USA Today*

The Sound of Music occupies such an exalted place in our affections that it's less a Broadway musical than a modern folk tale we all know by heart. So how could the slick new Broadway revival not be a success? Surprise! It's doomed from the get-go. ... Returning to Rodgers and Hammerstein's original — even with added songs written for the film — is like trading a Mercedes for a bicycle (2½ stars out of four).

Jeffrey Lyons, NBC-TV

The Sound of Music is back, and for a little while, all seems right with the world.

Dennis Cunningham, CBS-TV

It's a show of many charms, sweet, lovely and melodic. Rebecca Luker is a low-wattage Maria. ... It's all very harmless and mostly lightweight stuff with some fetching tunes. ... and oh my, is it cute. ... Still, for many, it's a much beloved musical, so though I wouldn't actually urge anyone to rush off to see this revival, neither would I try to stand in anyone's way.

Jacques Le Sourd, Gannett Newspapers

The Captain is a stiff. Maria is a bore. But the music sounds pretty good, and some of the kids are cute. (The others are ripe for strangling.). ... Don't bother with this anemic stage version, which is only technically "live" at $75 a ticket. Just rent the 1965 movie with Julie Andrews, or wait for the annual network broadcast. That, at least, is free.

Joan Hamburg, WOR-Radio

Get tickets! We came out happy as larks. So if you want to feel good, at a time when we are besieged by smut everywhere ... see something that rings as true as it ever did, and come out singing.

Vincent Canby, *The New York Times*

Was it not Oscar Hammerstein's grandfather who remarked, years back, "No way can you force an audience to go to something they don't want to"? ... The news this morning: *The Sound of Music* still isn't about to disappear, certainly not when it is done with the skill evident in the revival.

From the Advertisement for the Martin Beck Theatre

It was really, really good. The kids and the music are terrific! [Eliza Lewine, age 9]

I loved it! The show was incredible! Maria and all were good! [Danielle Raso, age 11]

They love this show everywhere.

Asia? They perform *The Sound of Music* in Beijing, where it has been translated into Chinese.

The Middle East? "You know, the biggest laugh I've had in some time," said Anna Crouse, "is over some producer, who shall be nameless, who put the show on in Israel. And I blew my top, because the cuts he'd made in the script were simply appalling. I protested! I thought: money isn't that important that we have to ruin this show. So the Rodgers & Hammerstein Organization got to him, and he responded, 'Well, in the first place, it's too long; nobody in Israel wants to stay in the theatre after 10 p.m. and nobody in Israel wants to know about nuns and Nazis.' So I asked, 'Tell me, what's left?'"

And on and on, all over the globe.

Even as the phenomenon continues, our tale ends here.

Let it suffice to explain the appeal of *The Sound of Music*, and, for that matter, of *Oklahoma!*, the two greatest hits of the immortal collaboration of Richard Rodgers and Oscar Hammerstein — be they on Broadway, or on the wide screen, or in a theatre of your choosing — let it suffice for us simply to quote the title Hammerstein wrote for a song in their final show: "No Way to Stop It"!

Appendix: Production Notes by Ken Bloom

PRODUCTION: Broadway

Theatre: Lunt-Fontanne Theatre

Dates: November 16, 1959 – June 15, 1963
Number of Performances: 1,443
Produced by Leland Hayward, Richard Halliday, Messrs. Rodgers
    and Hammerstein
Directed by Vincent J. Donehue
Musical numbers staged by Joe Layton
Settings by Oliver Smith
Costumes by Lucinda Ballard
Miss Martin's clothes by Mainbocher
Lighting by Jean Rosenthal
Music director, Frederick Dvonch
Orchestrations by Robert Russell Bennett
Choral arrangements by Trude Rittman

CAST

Maria Rainer, Mary Martin
The Mother Abbess, Patricia Neway
Captain Georg Von Trapp, Theodore Bikel

Children:
Liesl, Lauri Peters
Friedrich, William Snowden
Louisa, Kathy Dunn
Kurt, Joseph Stewart
Brigitta, Marilyn Rogers
Marta, Mary Susan Locke
Gretl, Evanna Lien
Rolf Gruber, Brian Davies
Elsa Schraeder, Marion Marlowe
Max Detweiler, Kurt Kasznar

MUSICAL NUMBERS

ACT I

Scene One – Nonnberg Abbey
Preludium, Nuns

Scene Two – Mountainside Near the Abbey
The Sound of Music, Maria

Scene Three – The Office of the Mother Abbess, the Next Morning
Maria, Mother Abbess, Sisters Margaretta, Berthe, Sophia
My Favorite Things, Maria and Mother Abbess

Scene Four – A Corridor in the Abbey
Scene Five – The Living Room of the Trapp Villa
Do-Re-Mi, Maria and Children

Scene Six – Outside the Trapp Villa, That Evening
Sixteen Going on Seventeen, Liesl and Rolf

Scene Seven – Maria's Bedroom
The Lonely Goatherd, Maria and Children

Scene Eight – Hallway in the Trapp Villa

Scene Nine – Terrace of Trapp Villa, Six Weeks Later
How Can Love Survive? Elsa, Max, Captain
Reprise, *The Sound of Music*, Maria, Captain, Children

Scene Ten – Hallway in the Trapp Villa

Scene Eleven – The Living Room
Laendler, dance by Maria and Captain
So Long, Farewell, Children

Scene Twelve – A Corridor in the Abbey

Scene Thirteen – The Office of the Mother Abbess, Three Days Later
Climb Ev'ry Mountain, Mother Abbess

ACT II

Scene One – The Terrace
No Way to Stop It, Captain, Max, Elsa
An Ordinary Couple, Maria and Captain

Scene Two – A Corridor in the Abbey, Two Weeks Later

Scene Three – The Office of the Mother Abbess

Scene Four – A Cloister Overlooking the Chapel
Processional, Ensemble
Reprise, *Maria*, Ensemble

Scene Five – The Living Room, One Month Later
Reprise, *Sixteen Going on Seventeen*, Maria and Liesl
Reprise, *Do-Re-Mi*, Maria, Captain, Children

Scene Six – The Concert Hall, Three Days Later
Edelweiss, Captain, Maria, Children
Reprise, *So Long, Farewell*, Maria, Captain, Children

Scene Seven – The Garden of Nonnberg Abbey
Reprise, *Climb Ev'ry Mountain*, Company

PRODUCTION: Touring Company

Produced by Messrs. Rodgers and Hammerstein
Dates: 1961

CAST

Maria Rainer, Florence Henderson
The Mother Abbess, Beatrice Krebs
Captain Georg Von Trapp, John Myhers
Children
    Liesl, Imelda de Martin
    Friedrich, Ricky Wayne
    Louisa, Melanie Dana
    Kurt, Richard Carafa
    Brigitta, Nita Novy

Marta, Linda Ross
Gretl, Christopher Norris
Rolf Gruber, Peter Van Hattum
Elsa Schraeder, Lynn Brinker
Max Detweiler, Jack Collins

PRODUCTION: London

Theatre: Palace Theatre
Dates: May 18, 1961 – January 14, 1967
Number of Performances: 2,385
Produced by Williamson Music, Ltd.
Restaged by Jerome Whyte
Lighting by George Wright

CAST

Maria Rainer, Jean Bayless
The Mother Abbess, Constance Shacklock
Captain Georg Von Trapp, Roger Dann
Children:
    Liesl, Barbara Brown
    Friedrich, John Coxall
    Louisa, Janet Ware
    Kurt, John Bosch
    Brigitta, Susan Whitnell
    Marta, Ann Dyer
    Gretl, Melanie Parr
    Rolf Gruber, Nicholas Bennett
    Elsa Schraeder, Eunice Gayson
    Max Detweiler, Harold Kasket

PRODUCTION: Film Version

Dates: 1965
A Twentieth Century-Fox Production
Produced and Directed by Robert Wise
Screenplay by Ernest Lehman
Associate Producer, Saul Chaplin
Choreography by Marc Breaux and Dee Dee Wood
Production designed by Boris Leven
Costumes by Dorothy Jenkins

Music Director, Irwin Kostal
Orchestrations by Mr. Kostal

CAST

Maria Rainer, Julie Andrews
The Mother Abbess, Peggy Wood (sung by Margery McKay)
Captain Georg Von Trapp, Christopher Plummer (sung by Bill Lee)
Children:
    Liesl, Charmian Carr
    Friedrich, Nicolas Hammond
    Louisa, Heather Menzies
    Kurt, Duane Chase
    Brigitta, Angela Cartwright
    Marta, Debbie Turner
    Gretl, Kym Karath
    Rolf Gruber, Daniel Truhitte

MUSICAL NUMBERS

Cut from Broadway score: *How Can Love Survive?*; *No Way to Stop It*; *An Ordinary Couple*
Songs written for the movie: *I Have Confidence in Me*, Maria; *Something Good*, Maria and Captain

PRODUCTION: Broadway Revival

Theatre: Martin Beck
Dates: March 12, 1998 – June 20, 1999
Number of Performances: 533
Produced by Hallmark Entertainment, Thomas Viertel, Steven
    Baruch, Richard Frankel, Jujamcyn Theatres
Directed by Susan H. Schulman
Choreographed by Michael Lichtefeld
Settings by Heidi Ettinger
Costumes by Catherine Zuber
Lighting by Paul Gallo

CAST

Maria Rainer, Rebecca Luker
The Mother Abbess, Patti Cohenour
Captain Georg Von Trapp, Michael Siberry

Children:
    Liesl, Sara Zelle
    Friedrich, Ryan Hopkins
    Louisa, Natalie Hall
    Kurt, Matthew Ballinger
    Brigitta, Tracy Alison Walsh
    Marta, Andrea Bowen
    Gretl, Ashley Rose Orr
    Rolf Gruber, Dashiell Eaves
    Elsa Schraeder, Jan Maxwell
    Max Detweiler, Fred Applegate

SONGS

Added from film version: *I Have Confidence, Something Good*
Songs cut from original score: *Ordinary Couple*

Sources & Credits

PUBLISHED SOURCES

Dance to the Piper by Agnes de Mille, Da Capo, 1980.
The Dramatists Guild Quarterly, Summer, 1997.
Getting to Know Him by Hugh Fordin, Ungar, 1986.
The Golden Age of Movie Musicals by Saul Chaplin, University of Oklahoma Press, 1994.
"Interview with Mrs. Dorothy Rodgers," *The New York Times*, April 22, 1990.
Lyrics by Oscar Hammerstein II, Hal Leonard, 1985.
Lyrics by Lorenz Hart, Knopf, 1986.
Mister Abbott by George Abbott, Random House, 1963.
Musical Stages by Richard Rodgers, Random House, 1949.
My Heart Belongs by Mary Martin, William Morrow, 1976.
People Will Talk by John Kobal, Knopf, 1986.
"The Saga of the Ernest Lehman Screenplay," unpublished manuscript by Michael Mattesino, 1994.
The Street Where I Live by Alan Jay Lerner, W.W. Norton, 1978.
Take Them Up Tenderly by Margaret Case Harriman, Knopf, 1944.
Theatre in America by Mary C. Henderson, Abrams, 1989.
Theo: The Autobiography of Theodore Bikel, Harper Collins, 1994.
They're Playing Our Song by Max Wilk, Da Capo, 1997.
Twenty Best American Plays, 1918–1958, edited by John Gassner, Crown, 1961.
Underfoot in Show Business by Helene Hanff, Moyer Bell, 1989.
A Wayward Quest by Theresa Helburn, Little Brown, 1960.

ORAL HISTORIES

Philip Barry, Jr., Waterford, Connecticut
Theodore Bikel, New York

Jay Blackton, Los Angeles
George Church, Fort Myers, Florida
Saul Chaplin, Los Angeles
Anna Crouse, New York
Bambi Linn de Jesus, Massachusetts
Agnes de Mille, New York
Alfred Drake, New York
Leslie Epstein, Brookline, Massachusetts
Frank Goodman, New York
Hayes Gordon, Australia
William Hammerstein, Connecticut
Edmund Hartmann, Santa Fe, New Mexico
Leland Hayward, New York
Ethel Heyn, Westport, Connecticut
Celeste Holm, New York
George Irving, New York
Ernest Lehman, Los Angeles
Miranda Levy, Santa Fe, New Mexico
Lauri Peters, New York
Marc Platt, Florida
Harold Prince, New York
Paul Shiers, New Jersey
Vivian Smith Shiers, New Jersey
Elaine Scott Steinbeck, New York
Miles White, New York
Robert Wise, New York
Kate Friedlich Witkin, New York
Mary Hunter Wolfe, New Haven, Connecticut

CREDITS

Index

Fellini, Federico, 59
Fiddler on the Roof, 83
Field, Ron, 2
Fields, W. C., 78
"the first dollar," 56
First Impressions, 45
Flower Drum Song, 6, 11, 55, 61
Follies, 1
Fonda, Henry, 9
Fordin, Hugh, 43
Fosse, Bob, 2
Foxy, 2
Franklin, Myra, 79
Frankovich, Mike, 65
Freed, Arthur, 63
From the Terrace, 55

G

Gannett Newspapers, 90–91
Garbo, Greta, 9
Garland, Judy, 73
Gersh, Phil, 66
Gierasch, Stefan, 24
Gill, Brendan, 78
Gone with the Wind, 10, 11
Goodman, Frank, 8, 37, 52
Gorrin, Michael, 24
Green, Adolph, 6, 45
Griffith, Andy, 15
Guarin, Renée, 44
Guinness Book of Records, 47
Gypsy, 2, 10, 11, 15–16, 28

H

Halliday, Richard, 6, 7–10, 11, 18, 30,
    47, 51
Hallmark Entertainment, 86
Hamburg, Joan, 91
Hammerstein, Dorothy, 33
Hammerstein, James, 17
Hammerstein, Oscar, *see also* Rodgers
    and Hammerstein
    cancer and, 24–25, 32, 33
    critical reviews and, impact on, 39

death of, 43
"Edelweiss" and, 33–34
on future of American musicals, 4–5
imminent death of, preparations
    for, 43
lyric work and, 17–18
success of *The Sound of Music,*
    confidence in, 39, 42
Hammerstein, William, 18
Harrison, Rex, 57, 65, 69
The Hasty Heart, 11
"I Have Confidence," 72–73, 74
"I Haven't Got a Worry in the World," 43
Hayes, Helen, 7
Hayward, Leland, 6, 9–10, *10,* 11, 15–16,
    28, 30, 33, 51, 54
Helburn, Theresa, 8
Henderson, Florence, 28, 49
Hepburn, Audrey, 69–70
Hepburn, Katharine, 9
Herald Tribune, 38
Herald-Tribune, 78
Hersey, John, 9
High Button Shoes, 2
Hitchcock, Alfred, 55
Hobson, Harold, 53, 79
Holliday, Judy, 3
"Honey Bun," 5
Howard Johnson's, 55
"How Can Love Survive?", 72

I

Imperial Theatre, 2

J

Jolson, Al, 2
Journal-American, 39

K

Kael, Pauline, 78, 79
Kander, John, 87
Kaplan, Mike, 76
Kasznar, Kurt, 24, *34*

N

Nazis, 7, 8, 13, 24, 31, 32, 54, 63–64, 67,
83, 87–88
NBC Television, 90
Mary Martin's contract with, 8–9, 46
"spectaculars," 7, 8
Neway, Patricia, 28, 29, 32
New Dramatists, 3, 4, 5
New Yorker, 78, 79
The New Yorker, 52
The New York Post, 89–90
The New York Times, 77–78, 89, 91
Nixon, Marni, 69, 73
Nonnberg Abbey, 70, 88
North by Northwest, 55
Norton, Eliot, 32, 39
"No Way to Stop It," 72

O

Oklahoma!, 1, 4, 13–15, 83
One Touch of Venus, 5
Operettas, 1
"An Ordinary Couple," 16, 72

P

Pacific 1860, 5
Pajama Game, 3
Palace Theatre, 53–54, 79
Paramount, 7, 8
Paris Herald, 78
Parsons, Louella, 70
"The Perfect Fool," 2
Peter Pan, 6, 8, 9, 46
Peters, Lauri, *41–42,* 45–46, *48*
Pinza, Ezio, 5–6
Pipe Dream, 6
pitch-meetings, 62
Plaza Hotel, 43
Plummer, Christopher, 71–72, 79–80
Porter, Cole, 2, 3, 5, 83
Post, 39
"Preludium," 85
Prince, Harold, 2
The Prize, 59

R

Radio City, 9
Randolph, John, 24
Reiner, Maria, 8, 16, 17, 18, 70
Ritchard, Cyril, 6
Ritz-Carlton, 34
Rivoli Theatre, 77
Robbins, Jerome, 2, 5, 6, 15
Roberts, Rachel, 65
Rodgers, Richard, *22,* 30, *76, see also*
Rodgers and Hammerstein
Laura Peters hired by, 45
on Martin, 47
Plaza meeting with Oscar
Hammerstein and, 43
songs for film version written by,
72–73
Yale Daily News pan and, annoyance
with, 31
Rodgers and Hammerstein, *17, see also*
Hammerstein, Oscar; Rodgers,
Richard
critical reviews of, 32
final collaboration of, 14
influence of, on American musical, 4
Lindsay and Crouse and, give-and-
take process between, 16
score to *The Sound of Music* and, 11
South Pacific and, 5–6
success of, 3–4
Twentieth Century-Fox partnership
and, 54
Rogers, Marilyn, *48*
Roman Holiday, 62
Romeo and Juliet, 5
Rosary College, 18
Rosenfeld, Jonas, 77, 78
Round Hill, 17

S

Sabrina, 55
St. James Theater, 14
St. Louis Municipal Opera, 1
"A Salute to France" festival, 7
Salzburg, 13, 15, 31, 70, 73–74, 87–88

About the Author

Max Wilk has conducted a not-so-private affair with American show business for more than seven decades.

It began with silent movies (yes, he's that old!), Broadway musical comedies, vaudeville (until Vitaphone buried that art form), and then the all-talking, all-singing, and all-dancing movies that followed. When radio took over in the 1930s, he was a dedicated fan, and when television killed radio in the 1940s, he was there to move into that exciting new business as a writer and producer.

Along the way, somehow he's found time to write radio and TV scripts, revue sketches, screenplays, and magazine articles. Novels, yes, and nonfiction, and he's even committed the ultimate madness, Broadway plays and two musicals!

If you are under forty, you will be delighted to know him as the author of the book of the Beatles' *Yellow Submarine*.

While you go to the beach in the summer, Wilk goes to the Eugene O'Neill Playwrights Conference, at Waterford, Connecticut, and works there as a dramaturge (don't ask what that word means) with aspiring playwrights.

But enough biography. The important thing about his books, of which this is the twenty-fourth, is that they are filled with facts, truth, anecdotes, and pure entertainment, proof of Wilk's lifelong love affair with our American show business.

And now, the house lights are going down, the overture is about to begun. Turn back to page 1, and join the rest of the audience. Enjoy!